Kids' Bedtime Meditation

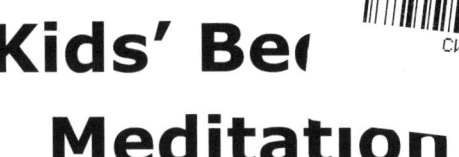

Let your Kid feel Happy and Calm into a Fantastic World. A Mindful and Relaxing Night-Night Stories to Help Children Fall Asleep Fast (with Kids' Mindfulness Exercises).

Mindfulness Wellbeing Team

© **Copyright 2019 - All rights reserved.**

The content contained within this book may not be reproduced, duplicated or transmitted without direct written permission from the author or the publisher.

Under no circumstances will any blame or legal responsibility be held against the publisher, or author, for any damages, reparation, or monetary loss due to the information contained within this book. Either directly or indirectly.

Legal Notice:

This book is copyright protected. This book is only for personal use. You cannot amend, distribute, sell, use, quote or paraphrase any part, or the content within this book, without the consent of the author or publisher.

Disclaimer Notice:

Please note the information contained within this document is for educational and entertainment purposes only. All effort has been executed to present accurate, up to date, and reliable, complete information. No warranties of any kind are declared or implied. Readers acknowledge that the author is not engaging in the rendering of legal, financial, medical or professional advice. The content within this book has been derived from various sources. Please consult a licensed professional before attempting any techniques outlined in this book.

By reading this document, the reader agrees that under no circumstances is the author responsible for any losses, direct or indirect, which are incurred as a result of the use of information contained within this document, including, but not limited to, — errors, omissions, or inaccuracies.

Table of Contents

Table of Contents 3

Introduction 5

How to Teach Kids Bedtime Meditation 8

Mindfulness & Relaxation Exercises for Kids 15

Hilda's Mermaid 30

The Poppies 35

The Fairies and the Dandelion 40

The Pink and Blue Eggs 44

The Wise Old Gander 48

Dinah Cat And The Witch 54

The Star and The Lily 59

Lazy Gray 64

The Old Gray Hen 68

The Worsted Doll 73

The Good Sea Monster 83

Mother Turkey and Her Chicks 87

Tearful 92

Where The Sparks Go 97

Mr. 'Possum 101

The Rooster That Crowed Too Soon 106

The Mirror's Dream 110

The Disorderly Girl 114

The Shoemaker Rat 118

The Contest 122

Why The Morning-Glory Sleeps 127

Dorothy and The Portrait 132

Snow-White and Rose-Red 137

Mistress Pussy's Mistake 142

KID 145

Little China Doll 151

Going Forward - Activating Your Parenting Imagination ... 154

Conclusion 160

Introduction

I want to start by thanking you for downloading this awesome guide – "***Kids' Bedtime Meditation***."

The subject meditation is a broad one and many people find it difficult to define the term. It has been mistakenly misunderstood and misused, most especially by the media culture. However, there is no reason to complicate the answers when trying to define meditation.

In simple terms, meditation is a methodology you can follow to help deal with certain medical conditions, stress, and anxiety through thinking, contemplation and reflection. It is a unique way that calms the mind and frees us from doubts, anxiety, judgment and, in other words, beyond our mental state. This state of consciousness goes beyond the usual awakening.

Meditation is a means of understanding and experiencing the inner knowledge center. It is not a religion, though it plays a role in the wisdom of the whole world. Meditation is a science. This means that it has defined the principles that a particular process exists and after that, and the results can be confirmed.

In Yoga (Ashtanga Yoga) the word for meditation is Dhyana, and not meditation or imagination.

The practice of meditation is to clear the mind, to allow to keep calm and to meditate. Today, in the modern world, most of us are already used to focusing on the external world for all our educational practices, instead of looking within. Meanwhile, when there is silence everywhere and the mind falls silent, without any distraction, your meditation gets deeper.

Meditation is a state of regenerative awareness. Your mind is clear, you are fully awake, but your mind is not focused on the external environment or any of the happenings around. You are cultivating a one-way inner state that will allow the mind slip into silence with much more ease.

Having understood the nitty-gritty of meditation, let's proceed to learn how bedtime meditation can help your kids. Evidently, when you think of the term bedtime, pictures of fluffy pillows and crisp white sheets fill our mind. We think of lying in bed, sipping a glass of warm milk, and perhaps, reading a book. As parents with young children, it's possible these pictures aren't so clear in your head.

Bedtime can be the most taxing part of one's day. And kids see the bedtime as the perfect time for them to settle down and get ready for sleep. The kids also see the bedtime as a great game that involves jumping and playing on the couch, listening to stories, going to the bathroom several times, playing with their noisiest toys and in general becoming over-excited.

Some of the stories I have listed was always a part of my sleeping routine, and they suddenly make me reflects the day I had each of my kid. Lately, I HAVE BECOME MORE COMMITTED TO THE meditation thing for my kids. I found that it helps visualize them for yourself instead of being passive.

I want to urge you to read these stories I have shared in this special guide. These recordings have been so helpful to the children themselves, I thought that I share them with you mothers and fathers. So, relax while you meditate with your children (ideal for children between 4 and 10 years old) and see how they respond to them. By the way, sweet dreams!

Let's begin!

How to Teach Kids Bedtime Meditation

All forms of meditation fall into two basic categories. There is a form of mindfulness meditation and then mindfulness meditation. These two techniques are opposite the end of the spectrum of meditation.

Mind meditation is the practical cleansing of the mind, of witnessing and transcending the mind. Examples of this type of meditation are Buddhist meditation and TM meditation. Focused meditation is the practice of using the mind as a tool for self-healing and internal transplantation. You practice this type of meditation when you are involved in creative visualization, guided images and breathing exercises. Mindfulness-centered meditation is best for children because it allows the child to practice mindfulness through focused and physical relaxation.

As parents, we can start practicing meditation with our children, usually from 4 years old. This constant practice allows your little one to transform meditation into an integral and natural part of his daily life, even during adulthood.

Teaching children is different from teaching adults. Children have less patience, less distance and less ability to sit. On the other hand, they have a more amazing imagination, a feeling of joy and learn, for example.

Why is meditation so important in our lives? Children are constantly exposed to violent media, peer pressure, billboards, sexually explicit images and interpretation, noise pollution, air pollution, chemicals, unhealthy food with chemicals and school deadlines, all of which causes stress on the body and minds. Meditation is an important practice to maintain children's balance and ability to cope with stress. As they slowly and slowly find themselves there, children feed themselves with a healthy sense of themselves and, therefore, improve their self-esteem.

Children in each situation will feel a sense of personal power and the ability to defend themselves. You can experience the world apart from a chaotic and winding world of needs and needs. Creating this space for our children to experience relaxation and self-esteem improves the feeling of happiness and the inner understanding that they can really do what they have in mind.

As a result, to teach children meditation effectively, keep the following six principles in mind.

Make it Attractive and Fun

The most important thing when teaching children to meditate is to present forms in a more attractive, fun and attractive way. Never let them get bored. I love that it is a fun activity (like a game) and children have to try again.

The principle of "making it fun" means that you should choose techniques that are naturally appealing to children, such as working with their senses and imagination. It also means that you have to adjust the meditation guidelines to make them more attractive.

For example, instead of asking children to "watch you breathe," you can ask them to put a small toy in their belly and drag it up and down. Have them try to move the toy as slowly as possible.

You go there, you just give them a deep breath and don't even notice it! Of course, this approach depends on age. Is your "student" a child (6-9), between (14-14) or a teenager (14-17)? The way you teach a 5-year-old is different from the way you portray an 11-year-old. This meditation training for children needs to apply these principles and techniques to the child's age and personality.

Appeal to Their Imagination

It is difficult for most children to understand abstract concepts. Instead, children enjoy activities that allow them to use their imagination and creativity. So, make sure you involve your imagination in action.

One way to do this is to frame meditation as a challenge. You have to communicate with your creativity and imagination, and that depends a lot on the child. For example: physical rest is a strong door to meditation. When you teach it, you present it as a challenge: "Let's play a game called Buddha Statue. We sit in this special position, pretending to be a statue and slowly increasing from 100 to 100. If you go before that, you are lost."

If your child loves action movies, he can create a metaphor like this: "Your soul is like a secret stealthy agent that sometimes wants to disappear. Your mission is to protect him, so follow him in a careful and silent manner. However, be so careful because he could take to his heels in blink of an eye.

Create an Atmosphere of "Lovely Meditation"
Another way is to create an atmosphere of "lovely meditation" at home or at school. Children like to move to another world with different experiences and strange objects. You can say something like: a sacred space, a magical space, and when you enter and follow the meditation, all your things disappear and you feel very relaxed and happy.

Keep It Short
Children do not have to wait 20 minutes on the floor. Therefore, keep the exercise short, especially for children

under 10 years. You should never get tired of exercise, but leave the feeling that you want to "want more."

A general guideline is to hold meetings until the child's age, plus one. So, if your child is 8 years old, do the session for a maximum of 9 minutes. To make it more fun, you can use a ring timer program.

Lead for Example
Children learn more by following the instructions below. They like to imitate adults and feel old. Therefore, the best way to teach a child to meditate is to meditate! All areas are striking, so be sure to give a solid example of how to integrate meditation into your daily life.

Let your child feel still while meditating. Finally, he will ask you what you did and then it will be time to teach them. Otherwise, he will increase his curiosity by saying something like: "This is a special exercise that only adults can do, but if you have a good week, I can teach you on Saturday."

Do you want your children to meditate? Be an example.

It also means that you have to meditate with them. Do you want them to be regular in their training? You need to regulate yourself and make meditation a family practice.

Be Flexible and Supportive
At the end of the exercise together, ask them how their experience was. This would be a good plan to draw them what

their meditation session is, the experience they have experienced or the "before and after" drawing. This encourages children to express themselves.

Then, confirm what they share. Accept what the child says, even if it is exaggerated, because we leave room for imagination. If you lead a group of children, reaffirm everyone's experiences and make sure that no child is confused, lost or unhappy about it.

Start with Five Minutes of Relaxation at Bedtime

With five minutes to rest at bedtime is easy. The stories presented in the following chapters will help you get started. Create a short break in bed using your imagination and genius to ask your child to imagine a sun just above their head, eliminating stress or worry. This will make your body very calm and relaxed.

Continue with the details of the relaxation waves above and above the body to touch and relax any muscle and body. Children find this very relaxing. It also helps build a close family bond by spending more time with your baby in a relaxed and enjoyable time.

Teach your child to count from ten to one and rest as much as possible, let all worries disappear. Bring an animal friend to your stage or a lovely cloud where your child can enter. Help your child relieve stress one by one by pressing stress on a nearby balloon and observing the stress and worry of POPs.

There are no infinite possibilities for your stories. Your own living imagination makes these possibilities unlimited.

This focused approach helps children in a variety of ways. Children can concentrate better, feel more balanced in their daily lives, are calmer and more comfortable. If we do not teach our children meditation and tranquility, they become a collection of nervous and unhappy energy. Children desperately need a way out of their stress. 69% of children under 10 have trouble sleeping and 76% of school-age children are worried. As responsible parents, we can provide such tools to our children to help them fully realize their life potential.

Mindfulness & Relaxation Exercises for Kids

Anyone who has children or deals with them knows that the most difficult thing is to force them to sit and rest. It is understandable, of course, that they are just beginning to experience the world and are eager to do everything possible. But unfortunately, modern society has made this energy too unrealizable and aimed at making it more productive.

Life in our society is like living in a circular tricycle with lights, shows, games and attractions that are constantly blinking. How can we expect our children to feel silent and meditate? Relaxation exercises are easy for children and teenagers, but difficult to apply because our children don't feel enough to try them.

This is the age of technology and our children understand it above what we usually do, if we want to give them the joy of silence and beauty, then we have to take them in a way that has nothing to do with them. The way we learned it. Of all the relief workouts for young people and teenagers, the most productive is meditation in terms of greater concentration and concentration.

Of course, when we think of meditation, we immediately think of sitting in a quiet room with our eyes closed or on a rock and listening to the sound of a river. I am a father and I know that the small possibility that meditation likes is not small at all. However, a quick search in the schoolyard can show you the solution. Children use them all the time as a way to adapt to the world, and now they can use them as a way to adapt them – headphones.

Relaxation is related to our thoughts directly. Have you ever felt deeply relaxed while dealing with anxiety or other stressful thoughts?

It is essential to add information on how to grow positively for your child's relaxation and physical training. Because of the flexibility of the brain, the ability of the brain to grow and change continuously based on our use over time, it is especially important that we support children in creating positive thinking patterns early in life. These patterns can be real-life passages, real passports to relax along those intense roads and storms that cross life.

Next, we will look into mindfulness and relaxation exercises you can do with kids.

Binaural Meditation

You have probably heard that meditation has important physiological, psychological and spiritual benefits and you would like to start. There are many meditation techniques that have been developed over the years and if you spend enough time learning and practicing, they can all be effective. Binaural meditation is a technology that helps the meditation process and makes it easier for children to learn and develop.

Each type of meditation is designed to relieve stress and anxiety and reduce brain wave activity in the slower alpha and theta frequency bands. During the day, the brain generally operates in the high frequency beta domain.

Binaural meditation is an excellent way to take your children to a quieter mood, even if you know it. All they know is that they listen to lovely music and it gives you a sense of peace.

Binaural meditation is a technological way of listening to a particular sound that is heard while using headphones. To help the brain, they set the frequency level of their brain waves from the active beta mode to the alpha and theta meditation ranges. This makes it very necessary to achieve meditation and concentration. Loading binaural rhythms helps you a lot, so you don't have to work hard to meditate.

If you want to start practicing meditation, try binaural meditation. Both phones can be easily downloaded online.

They are easy to use and make meditation more enjoyable and valuable.

They have no way of knowing that the use of sound frequencies is balancing both hemispheres of their brains and, therefore, balancing their thoughts and lives. They still have the same passion and energy, but use them to direct their focus and attention in the present moment. They will learn to appreciate their minds and, through them, their lives.

During meditation, you try to slow the baby's brain and turn off the constant "talk" that is turned off. Like most of us, we are constantly thinking about the problems at work, the housework we have to do, the things that children need and look for. This training will take enough concentration and concentration to close the door to this noise and reach those areas of meditation.

If your children have enough meditation, you can do it. But if they can't get enough exercise and want faster results, the solution is binaural meditation.

Sound Meditation (Hearing)
Sound meditation encourage the child to use the sense of hearing as a door to the gift, be open and relaxed here and now. It helps create impartial awareness and awareness of mental stagnation.

- Close your eyes and take a deep breath.
- Imagine that your ears get too big. It is as big as your body. They can hear everything.
- Observe the sounds you hear in your room. Stay with each music for a few seconds and then move on to the next.
- Then start listening to sounds far and wide. See how you can go now.
- Just leave the sound, don't think about it or call it that. Their ears do not hear any sound and do not like or hate them.
- Now see if you can hear the sound of your breathing. Listen to your soul music moment by moment.

Play a Musical Story

Put on a piece of music and have the children listen carefully and imagine what the story is about. In the end, ask them to share their stories.

Playing a musical story will help to develop your child's school of thought and abstract thinking.

Sound Concentration

Play the accompanying piece of music and ask the child to choose one of the instruments and only follow the sounds, exclusively.

Sound concentration develop the ability to focus on distraction.

From Sound to Silence
- Close your eyes and pay attention to the sounds you hear.
- Now listen carefully to the ear of the bowl. [Hit a bowl]
- Turn on the music in silence. See how long you can continue before it runs out. Try to find the last moment when the furtive sound of escape escapes silence.
- Now listen to the silence.

The coach repeats the process several times. It is great for calming down the child, and sharpening their sense of hearing.

Mantra Meditation (Hearing)
- The world mantra has a profound effect on the mind, largely due to the prolonged "mm" sound. It can even make your baby sleep.
- Close your eyes. Take a deep breath through your nose.
- Slowly sing OOMMM while breathing.
- At first, it is tall and then slowly softens and softens until exhaustion ends.
- Many Repeat the process over and over again, take a deep breath and sing while OM breathes.
- With each breath, try to make the OM sound longer and softer.
- Then close your mouth and repeat OM in your mind. Repeat once during breathing and once during breathing.
- Breathe and repeat the mantra meditation for the rest.

- You may want to skip steps 6 and 7 with younger children and keep it repeating the song.

Mantra meditation has a profound effect on mental, bodily and emotional peace. Integrate talk, listen and breathe and gives you a feeling of satisfaction. If performed in a group setting, you can create a strong bond between the students who sing together.

Gazing Meditation (Sight)

Darken the room, close all windows (so there is no breeze) and light a candle. This diverse environment, together with the fact that most children love fire, makes it a fun activity for them.

- Sit two or three feet away from the candle.
- Open your eyes and gently look (not force or look). Keep your eyes on the flame, while the hawk looks at its prey. Move your eyes neither to the left nor to the right, neither up nor down.
- After two minutes, close your eyes and look at the candle from beyond that may be in your mind.
- Play with that image: see if you can keep quiet in the center. Or try changing its size, color or brightness.
- After a while, open your eyes and look at the flame again. Then close your eyes and repeat the process.

Gazing meditation is a great practice to develop concentration, confidence and the ability to visualize.

Visualization Meditation (Sight)

Children generally have a better ability than adults. The key to making this meditation enjoyable is to allow them to choose their favorite object. Visualization Meditation (Sight) includes the following:

Blackboard design

- Close your eyes and imagine a blackboard in front of your eyes.
- Imagine the following words written on a blackboard. [Say some words and numbers, pausing between them.]
- Imagine dragging your favorite animal on a board. You have plaster pieces in many colors, so enjoy!
- Open your eyes and draw the animal on paper exactly as you had previously imagined.

Mental image

- Find a favorite toy, image or object and place it in front of you. [Mandala can also be used because children find it interesting and attractive.]
- For a minute, observe all the details of that object / toy.
- Close your eyes and visualize the object in front of you.
- After a while, open your eyes and take the second peak in the body.
- Close the eyes again and now try to visualize it in more detail in your mind.

Both methods increase children's ability to visualize. It also gives them more imagination and increases their focus.

Breath Mindfulness for Children

Breathing consciousness is the most popular form of meditation in Buddhism and the mental movement generates modern consciousness. Here are two simple ways to teach children.

Counting

- Close your eyes.
- Be aware of your breathing. You feel your abdomen or chest inhaling up and exhaling.
- Breathe mentally say "10". Breathe again Think "10". Then again "9" and "9". Then 8, 8 to 1,1.
- If you get lost, start again from 10. Your challenge is to reach 10 to 1 without forgetting your breathing.

Benefits: increases body awareness, concentration and relaxation.

Breathing Colors

Instead of counting your breath, imagine breathing in gold and pulling out the gray. When you breathe, the golden color fills your whole body with good things, happiness, relaxation, energy. Breathing, the gray color eliminates all bad things.

- Close your eyes and feel your whole body. Try to position your authority, the size it occupies in the room and feel its weight.
- Now imagine that your body is a mountain. As big as a mountain and as heavy as a mountain, it is firm and firm on the ground.
- Every time you breathe, you feel that your body is more like a mountain.
- Every time your body feels more relaxed and calm, you feel relaxed and calm too.
- Whenever you want to complete the meditation, after each inhalation, feel that your body returns to normal.

Breathing colors causes an improved effect on emotional well-being. It is ideal to calm, relax and increase body awareness. Also, good exercise for sleeping.

Space Travel (body)
- Close your eyes and lie down comfortably.
- Imagine that your body becomes very light. It is so light that it no longer weighs and begins to float up.
- Your body is light and transparent and floats in space. It leaves planet Earth, floating around the galaxy.
- Enjoy the way it feels light and free. Your mind also feels clear and open.
- After a while, start again on the floor and in the room where you are. Feel the body solidify again.

- Slowly move the toes and hands to finish the meditation.
- As a change, after step 4, you can make the child imagine that he is visiting another planet. This makes it look creatively different, what some children can enjoy. If you take this diversity, in the end, ask the child what the trip would be like and what the planet was like.

Space travel helps to relax and refresh. The problems and feelings are very low after this exercise. This is suitable for children with emotional disorders, too shy or sad.

Walking Beats Meditation (Body)

There are several types of walking meditation, most of which involve synchronizing slow steps with breathing or mantra. But what about children who are hyperactive and cannot do leisure walks?

Here is a way I created to help break up with energetic children. Put it as a challenge: "Let us see that you are committed to failure!".

- You need a metronome program (like this one) or a real metronome for this method.
- Set the metronome at a fast speed, such as 150 or 200 beats per minute. Have children walk (almost) with rhythms: every hit is a step.
- After one minute, reduce the speed and make the children realize and keep up.

- Reduce it to 30 beats per minute. At this point, children walk peacefully and peacefully.
- After a while, order them to synchronize their breathing with the steps, so that each breath takes two beats (4 seconds) and each breath leaves two beats.

Walking beats meditation is a method that is very dynamic and attractive. Expel these children from agitation.

Nidra Yoga for Children (Body)

A child will always remain fresh in his memory as the only moment in his life where he was free from stress, stress and worry, and the limited world around him would at least meet his needs. This is the period in which he develops his body and mind, and the moment in which his habits and lifestyle shape his future. When you are a child, you have energy, and unless your parents direct that energy in the right direction, you will eventually be a loser.

Children tend to be more focused than adults today. They are not upset about what they have done wrong in the past, and they are not worried about what they can do wrong in the future. In that sense, they are particularly good at learning to meditate.

Another benefit of children to adults is that they don't feel ashamed of trying something new. Adult students are difficult to teach how to use a shredder because sometimes they feel uncomfortable in the face or make noise in public. Not with children with more flexible minds, they are open to learning things that make them feel "great."

An ideal solution is to direct your child's energy towards early yoga to improve their discipline, self-discipline and self-esteem. As a result, the child improves communication skills, respect for others and love and concern for peers. Yoga at an early age shapes the harmony of a child's strength, flexibility and balance.

— **Memory and concentration in children**

You can improve focus and memory in children by practicing the composition of Oumkar songs, which even helps babies listen. Nidra yoga helps in the rapid secretion of growth hormone. Growth hormone plays an important role in the growth of the baby and Yoga Nidra plays an important role in the integration and strengthening of the various areas of the child's brain development. The balance also helps improve the concentration and memory of the baby.

— **Excessive energy levels in children**

Most children his age have extra energy, which they express with concern, and unless he guides them constructively, the child may have other problems. Proper breathing exercises provide adequate oxygen to the brain and cells of the baby's body and provide the needed relaxation.

— **Bad temper in children**

By breathing deeply, singing the Omkar action of Nidra Yoga can greatly help to solve children's problems, which parents consider strong, ephemeral and destructive to their desires. Even the group yoga practice strengthens the spirit of solidarity and teamwork. Create a spirit of respect and love among children.

Every mother wants her son to be tall and handsome. In yoga, modes such as triangles, warriors, mountains, tree pots and suriya burgers help increase a child's height and regularly stretch the spine and limbs of the child to improve flexibility. In addition, they also help increase calcium metabolism and its use in the body.

— **Respiratory problems**

Measured deep breathing exercises help increase oxygen to the brain and cells. In turn, this helps to maintain respiratory problems such as cough and cold, asthma, bronchitis and the like.

Teenagers can try some practical ways to imitate adults, but remember that there are special considerations for this age group. Nidra yoga is suitable for this age group and can use the form for adults. Teens are excellent at using visualization techniques, from the mental writing of the alphabet to building their own story.

Some of the most effective ways for teenagers are yoga self-awareness meditation. They can help teenagers with hormonal changes in their bodies and help calm their minds when dealing with relationships, school work or any stressful daily.

Children and adolescents suffer from anxiety, depression, stress and it is important that we teach them ways to reduce these conditions. Practicing mindfulness, like adults, is an effective way to do it right.

Hilda's Mermaid

Hilda's father was a small sailor and made long trips. Hilda lived in a small cabin on the beach, and while her father was away, she squirmed and knotted because her mother was dead and had to take home. Sometimes he took it out in a boat and fish, because Hilda liked water. He was born and always lived on the beach. When the water was very calm, Hilda looked into the deep blue and tried to see a mermaid. She was very anxious to see one, she heard her father tell such amazing stories about them: how they sang and combed their beautiful long hair.

One night, when the wind was raining and the rain was so strong in his window, Hilda heard the horn warning the sailors of the rocks. Hilda lit her father's big lantern and went down to the shore and hung it on the bevel gear there, so that the sailors wouldn't board their ships. Little Hilda was not afraid because she had seen such storms. When he returned to his hut, he realized that the door was inaccessible, but he thought the wind had opened it. When he arrived, he found a girl with beautiful hair sitting on the floor. At first, I was a little scared because the girl was wearing a green dress and wrapped it in the strangest way around her body.

The boy said, "I saw your light and it came in. The wind blew me up on the beach. I shouldn't have come in one night, but the big wave seemed so tempting that I thought of jumping and enjoying it. Take it, but the beach was closer to what I thought, and he took me right near his door. "

"Oh my God!" How Hilda's heart was beating because she knew that this baby must be a mermaid. Then he saw what he thought was a green dress wrapped around his body and tail, and his beauty fell on him like a lamp and shone.

"Do you want some of my dinner?" He asked Hilda why he wanted to be hospitable, although he had little idea of eating mermaids.

"Thank you," replied the siren. "I'm not very hungry, but if you could give me a seaweed sandwich, I'd love to."

Hilda didn't know what to do in vain, but she went to the closet and brought some bread, which she smeared with fresh and sweet butter and filled a glass with milk. She told him she was sorry, but she didn't have seaweed sandwiches, but she hoped she would love what she had prepared. The little mermaid ate it and Hilda was satisfied.

"Do you always live here?" He asked Hilda. "I think you'll be very warm and want to be part of the time in the water."

Hilda told him that he could not live like water in water because his body was not like him.

"Oh I'm very sorry!" The mermaid replied: "I expected you to come to me at some point; we had a great time, my sisters and I, under the sea."

"Tell us about your house," said Hilda.

"Come and sit with me, and I will be," he replied.

Hilda sat on the floor next to the floor. The mermaid felt Hilda's attire and thought she should wear a lot of clothes and bother.

"How can you swim?" She asked

Hilda told him to bring a swimsuit, but the mermaid thought it was a nuisance.

He said: "First I will tell you about our house." "Our father, Neptune, lives in a beautiful castle at the bottom of the sea. It is made of pearls. There are beautiful green things around the castle and there is good white sand around. All my sisters there live, and we are always happy to return home after being on top of the ocean, it's very cool in our house. The wind never blows there and the rain doesn't affect us. "

"You don't mind getting wet from the rain, right?" Hilda asked.

"Oh no!" The siren said: "But the rain hurts us. It falls on sharp points and feels like a pebble."

"How do you know how the stones are?" Hilda asked.

"Oh, sometimes the Nereids come and bother us, they throw stones and water so we can't see."

"Who are the nominees?" Hilda asked.

The mermaid said: "They are nymphs, but we make fish dogs get away with it. We are mermaids and they are very jealous of us because we are more beautiful than they are."

Hilda thought she was perfectly conceived, but the little mermaid seemed to be completely unaware that she had conveyed the idea.

"How do you find your way back home after being on top of the ocean?" Hilda asked.

"Oh, when Neptune's father tells us and finds all the missing ones, he sends the whale away. Sometimes he sends more than one.

"What do you eat besides seaweed sandwiches?" Hilda asked.

In response, the mermaid said: "very little fish and fish eggs." "We make cake when we have a party."

Hilda opened her eyes. "Do you have cake?" She asked.

"We do it. We chop the coral in the flour and mix it with the fish egg, then we put it in a shell and send a siren to the ocean," he said. And keeps it in the sun until it cooks. We collect the Persian Gulf and the grapes and we have seafood and lemonade to drink. "

"Lemonade?" Said Hilda. "Where do you get your lemons?"

"Why, lemon sea!" The mermaid replied: "This is a small mussel that has the color of a lemon."

"What do you do at your parties? Can't you dance?" Said Hilda.

"We swam with the music, turned it on and immersed ourselves.

"But music, where do you get music?" Hilda continued.

The siren replied: "We have a lot of music." "The sea elephant hits us; then there is the pipefish, the swordfish that scales the sea with its sword, the bubbles of the sea, and we all have splendid music. But it's late, and we have to do it again. Don't talk.

Then the little mermaid wrapped herself and soon fell asleep.

The sunlight in the window the next morning woke Hilda and looked at her. The mermaid wasn't there, but Hilda was sure it wasn't a dream, because she found seaweed on the ground, looking for her friend every time she went out in her boat, and when the whales hit, he knows they are telling fairies may they come home.

The Poppies

A long distance from here, in a far Eastern country, there once lived a very rich king. All kings are not rich, you know, but this one was, and his jewels were the most beautiful ever seen.

But this king dearly loved all the good things of this world and gave feasts and dances that lasted for days without any one sleeping. Of course, he could not lead such a life like that and have good health, and at last there came a time when the king could not sleep.

At last he offered a reward to anyone who could put him to sleep, no matter how it was accomplished. He said to the one who could do this he would give half his kingdom.

The poor king was the subject for many experiments, and when he had almost given up hope of ever sleeping again there came a strange-looking man to the gate of the castle. He wore a turban and a long, flowing robe of white, and wore around his neck many chains and strings of queer-looking beads.

"I can make the king sleep," he said, "but I must be allowed to have the grounds of the castle to myself and the king must obey me in every way."

The king was ready to do anything, and so the strange-looking man began his work, but before he would do anything for the king, he insisted upon having half the kingdom given into his hands, and when this was done, he set to work. No one was allowed to be near him, and the king was left alone in the castle with him.

One morning, not long after, the king saw what looked to be a sea of green all around the castle, but it really was a bed of green leaves, and soon there appeared white flowers among the leaves, and then the strange man told the king to walk among them.

Soon the king felt a drowsy feeling stealing over him, and he sat down in the midst of the sea of green and, in a few minutes, he was sound asleep.

Then the strange man began to repeat something in a sing-song tone and wave his hands over the sleeping king. He walked among the leaves and flowers, repeating his queer rhyme, and the leaves and flowers grew taller and taller until the king could not be seen, and the man moved away, still chanting:

"Poppy, poppy, flower of sleep,

Your drowsy spell around him keep,

For I can all his kingdom take if you do not let him wake."

The poppies grew until they reached the top of the castle, and everyone who went near to look for the king fell under the spell of their strange power until the people around gave it up and the strange man became king; he built a new castle and the old one was forgotten.

All went well with the new king until a young man called at his castle and asked him about the old king, and the servants told him how the strange flowers had grown around the castle and no one could go near, and that everyone thought that the old king was dead.

The new king, when he heard that the stranger was asking for the old king, had him driven from the castle.

"Tell your master," said the stranger to the servants, "that he will hear from me again."

The stranger went into the woods, where there lived an old witch, and at midnight they came out and went to the castle among the strange flowers.

The witch held her hands high over her head and waved them up and down, saying all the time:

"Poppy, poppy, sleepy flower,

Now I have you in my power.

I would have you shorter grow

Until the sleeping one you show."

Down came the tall flowers and bushes until the young man cried out, "Here he is," and then the flowers ceased to grow small. The witch knelt beside the sleeping king and whispered in his ear:

"Awake, good king, 'tis break of day,

And drive the false king far away."

The king opened his eyes and looked at the witch and the young man beside her. "What has happened?" he asked.

"I will leave you to tell him," said the witch. "The sun is up and I must go."

"When you offered to give half your kingdom to the one who could make you sleep," said the young man, "I set out for your castle with a box which contained a strange flower that had the power to make people sleep, but it had to be used with the greatest care, and I alone knew the secret of using it, for it was given to my grandmother by an old witch doctor.

"Before I could reach you, I was overtaken by a band of robbers and the box stolen. They told me what I intended to do with the pain of death, but I didn't tell the whole secret. Then they put me in a cave and rolled a stone in front of it that was too heavy to move and I left. I was almost dead from starvation when I was found by some peasants, who nursed me until I was well enough to travel, when I hurried here, only to find that one of the band of robbers had taken your whole kingdom after putting you to sleep with the charmed flower.

"He drove me from the castle when he heard that I was asking for you, and if it had not been for the witch who lives in the wood, I should not have been able to awaken you. She knew the secret, as she is the daughter of the witch who gave the flower to my grandmother."

When the king heard the strange story, he hurried with the young man to the castle where the robber king lived. He was asleep when they arrived, and the servants, who did not like their new master, ran out to meet the old king, and when they heard what had happened they went back to the castle and bound the robber while he slept, and when he awoke he was so frightened that he promised to tell where the rest of his band could be found if they would spare his life.

This they promised to do, and the country was rid of these bad men, for they were put on a ship and made to work the rest of their lives.

The king was so grateful to the young man who rescued him that he made him his heir, and when the king died, he left him his kingdom.

The Fairies and the Dandelion

The elves say that long ago the dandelion did not have the yellow flower or the fluffy white hat that was worn after removal.

They tell the story that the night before, while celebrating one of their country parties, there were cries and moans.

Queen Perry stopped dancing and listened. "It comes from the ground," he said. Among the grass. Hurry up, find everyone; find someone who is in trouble and come back and tell me.

Far from fairies and fields, gardens and streets. Upon arrival and among the blades of grass, they found strange weeds with leaves resembling a dandelion. They were crying and singing:

"Here we grow very bright and green,

The color of the grass, and cannot be seen.

Oh, bitter pain, but we don't stop

Until the fairies give us a yellow. "

He returned the fairies to his queen and told him what they had heard.

"If only they had asked for another color!" "There are a lot of yellow flowers now. If another yellow flower enters its bright circle, carrots, golden glitter and golden rods will be jealous. Come back and ask them if they give us whiteness," she said.

The elephants were crying with the queen's message, fleeing to the dandelions.

They said, "The queen will give you a white ball."

"No, no!" They cried "Yellow is the color we should use with our green leaves. This is the color of the sun and we want to get as close as possible." And everyone started crying:

"Oh, oh, we won't stop!

Until the fairies give us a yellow. "

They were so loud that Paris put her fingers in her ear as she returned to the queen.

The blades of grass grew taller and looked around. They said to the queen, "Turn off those noisy weeds." Give them the yellow they are crying and let them sleep. We are awake at sunset and will rise soon.

"What will we do?" The queen said. "I don't know where to get the yellow I want."

"If we could get some of the sun's rays, we could have exactly the color they were crying for," said one fairy. "Of course, we can't afford such a strong light, but the elves can for us to gather."

Then they went to see the elves and asked them to collect the sun's rays the next day and bring them to the valley the next night.

The elves were eager to help them, but the next day the sun was shining and they could only collect a few baskets of bright golden color.

When the queen saw the amount, she was disappointed. "This will never be a turnaround, and those who wear yellow shirts will cry louder than ever," he said. "Why don't we divide it between them?" Said Perry. "It will have little shelf life and we can give them our fluffy white hats when it's gone. We'll get them out soon and the dandelions can wear them for the rest of the season."

Queen's face lit up. "That is, if only the small, noisy weeds agreed. Go to them and tell them that if they want to accept our fluffy white hats, they can get the yellow they want most. Wear halfway through the season."

The fairies stormed the dandelions and told them what the queen had said. The dandelions did not cry, saying that you would be satisfied, and the queen passed on every golden grass on the grasslands, fields, gardens and trails.

The morning when the sun saw its bright color looking at him, he was surprised that he was almost silent.

The elephants kept their promise, and it was time to take off your fluffy white hoods, walk between the dandelions, and hang a hat on each stem.

The dandelions did not cry again, and the grass lay asleep from calm until sunrise.

The Pink and Blue Eggs

"I tell you I saw them with my own eyes," said the old white chicken, standing on one leg with her neck and beak open. "One was pink and the other was blue. They were just like any other egg, but the color, think about it, was the pink and blue egg. Who could have put them?" From another glance, the white hen looked at the group of hens and hens that surrounded her.

"Well, I know I didn't," said the stained chicken.

"You don't have to look at me," Brown said. "I've laid big white eggs, and you all know it. If I say this, the best eggs are in the yard."

"Oh, I wouldn't say that," White said. "He seems to have forgotten that the biggest egg ever laid in this yard was a little brown and white; the eggs are good, but they give me brown quality."

"You never put an egg on its size, but once," Brown Hun replied, "and everyone thought it was a weird egg, so the less you say it, the better I think "

"It's easy to understand how you feel about that egg, but it doesn't help us find out who laid the blue and pink eggs," White Hahn said.

"Where did you see it?" Asked the spotted chicken.

"On the table, next to the farm window," said the old white chicken. "I flew to the top of the barrel under the window and then stretched my neck and looked out the window. There, at the table, in a small basket, I saw those strange eggs." "Maybe the teacher bought them so that some of us would sit and be born," Brown said.

"Well, for my part I refuse to do that," White said. "I think it would be an insult to put those flashing things in our nests."

"I'm sure I won't hesitate," Speckled Hen said. "I was walking around here with a blue girl and a pink girl next to me and a spotted chicken next to me, looking funny.

"You didn't think for a minute that I would do that, I hope," Brown said. "I just mentioned the fact that the teacher might have such an idea, but I don't think about mixing colors. My little yellow creatures are not humiliated by a blue girl and the way they run. "

Speckled Hen said, "Maybe white is the color of henna." "The eggs he saw might be white."

"If you doubt my words or my look, go and get it yourself," White said. "You will find a blue egg and a pink egg, exactly as I told you."

Speckled Hen and Brown Hen escaped, followed by many more and all the girls in the yard.

One after another, they flew to the top of the barrel and looked out at the window of white eggs he had told them. Everything was right; the eggs were blue and pink.

"Tweet, tweet, tweet, tweet. We also want to see blue and pink eggs." We never saw them and we want to look at them. " "my God! Why did I talk to them before? "Brown said." They won't be silent unless they see, and how can I get them to that window? "" Have you ever thought not to cry at all? "Say white chicken." Say "no" once in a while; that's a lot of trouble."

"I have no tolerance for neglecting the little ones," Brown said as he walked his little son and tried to calm them down.

"Well, you better start now, because this is one of the things you can't do." White said he told Towser to tell the story of blue and pink eggs when picking up the dog home.

"If Master puts those eggs in one of our nests, wouldn't it be scary?" When he finished his story, he asked White Hahn.

"Oh, oh!" Towser laughed: "This is a good joke for you; when you see it, you don't know your eggs."

"Don't tell me I laid those colored eggs," White said, wondering if one of his companions was within earshot. "I know I have never done that."

"But you did it," Towser said with a smile. "I heard Master tell my little lover: 'If you want to paint eggs for Easter, take the ones that Van had laid. They are not as big as the others, and I cannot sell as well.'"

"Towser, if you never mention what you told me, I tell you that I saw a big bone this morning," White said. "I would keep this for myself. I would love to be chosen from time to time, but if you promise to hide what you just told me, you should have it."

Towser promised, and White Hen showed where he was hiding.

A few days after Brown said, "I don't know who the teacher wants to get those fancy eggs. If he leaves her at home, nobody can hatch them again."

"Oh, I forgot to tell you that those eggs were not really real eggs, but only Easter eggs for Master's girl, so we all worried nothing," White Han said. But tell her no, but don't tell her, because I didn't let them worry and I didn't know they were just eggs, they believed in; he thinks he's very wise, you know, you never do it to let him know how they cheated us."

The Wise Old Gander

There used to be a farmer who was not a good caregiver. He had no house for birds, birds and goats, and Old Fox, who lived in a cavity on the hill, never had trouble getting a beautiful goose or fat chicken for his dinner or breakfast.

"Something must be done at once," said Madam Goose. "There will be no one left in the whole yard if this keeps on. Why, only last night Madam Gray Hen was carried off and she has left all those little chicks; it is really too awful to think of."

"But what can we do?" asked Gray Goose. "The rooster does not know, for I heard one of his family ask him, and he only said the master should take better care of us."

"So, he should," replied Madam Goose, "but he doesn't, so we must care for ourselves unless we wish to be carried off, too. Let us go to the gander; he may be able to help us."

"Come with us," they called to the rooster and black men who were talking together; "we are going to see the gander and ask him to help us to be rid of Old Fox over the hill."

The gander stretched out his neck and blinked his eyes as he listened to their tale of woe.

"You are right, something must be done," he said; "and you are quite right in coming to me also. I will think over the matter and give you my advice later."

"Later!" screamed Madam Goose. "Later there will be no need for advice; there will be no one to give it or to advise. What we need is advice at once, and something that will rid us of Old Fox under the hill. He is eating the whole yard, one by one."

"Well, well," answered the gander, standing on one foot and then on the other. "I will think over the matter for a short time and then tell you my decision. You know, my dear madam, that great minds must have quiet to think out important matters. Leave me, I beg of you all, for a little while."

As soon as the port was alone, you would turn the pig. I said: "Mr. Pig," I would like to ask for your advice. The old fox on the hill kills all the birds and something must be done. "

"Oh, oh," he complained to the pig. "I can tell you what scares him. I stay up at night and drown in it; it's better than knowing where I am."

"Thank you, thank you, Mr. Pig." "I will tell my friends and I am sure they will feel safe at night."

"Your colleague is charged," Mr. Pig said. "I guess scaring that fox would be more than a nuisance."

Then he went to the donkey. "He doesn't think," he is very wise, but sometimes those with less wisdom speak wisely without knowing it.

"Mr. Donkey, I have asked for your advice. Old Fox is killing our chickens and geese. Something must be done to stop him, or no one will stay soon."

The donkey said, "Take off, do it. I see, Mr. Gander." "You have come to the right place for the consultation. Now go back to your friends and tell them you are not afraid; I will take care of the matter."

"But what are you going to do?" The giant asked.

"Why, my dear lord, I want to eat at Old Fox when I eat. I want to overwhelm him, and you will discover that he won't stay long when he hears my order."

"Oh, how can I thank you?" Said the belt, walk. "I will tell my friends immediately to take care of them until the night."

"Stupid old donkey," he complained. "I guess Old Fox has already heard of a hook before. Then I'll try the cow."

"Miss Cow, Old Fox releases all the chickens one by one, and if something is done at the same time to stop her, none of us will stay. What do you advise?"

"Oh, don't ask me, Mr. Gander," said the cow. "All I can do is rebel, and Old Fox doesn't think it more than the wind. I wish I was wise enough to advise him, but I am not."

"Thank you, Miss Cow," she said. "Thank you, Miss Cow." "You may have news of me. We can never say when we will need the help of our friends."

The next person he visited was the cat.

"Can you help me, Miss Puss?" The giant began. "We have all the birds in trouble; Old Fox takes one or more of us every night and we must do something to stop it all at once."

The cat shook his mouth and yawned, wondering if he was wise, asking for advice.

But Puss shut his mouth with a snap and sat down.

"Of course, I can help you," he said. "Have you ever seen my claws?"

The goose was back when Jack kept them in his eyes.

Goose confessed that he didn't, and Puss continued, "Well, leave it to me to protect the pen; this rover dog never seems to think of anything other than eating and sleeping. Talk again, scream and spit. And I can tell you and your friends that he won't come back. "

The goose said, "Thank you, thank you, Miss Cat."

"My God, but it was a narrow escape for me!" Said the goose. "He looks very positive when he opens his mouth. It seems like I'm getting advice, but it's not the kind to save my friends; they all feel confident that they can scare the old Fox," he said. "But neither of them can; I don't know. I don't know them all together …"

The goose stopped and raised his head. "I have it, I have this program; I will bring them all together and all do their part. I think we can scare Old Fox forever and ever," he said.

The goose went to the dog and he promised to bark. "Of course, we don't need to be close to others if we do that," the dog said. "But if you want to bring them in, every little help."

That night, donkeys, dogs, cats, cows and pigs met in the hallway. Everyone protested that others were not needed, all except cattle. He was temperate and said it would help. Then the rooster came in and offered to read it and the geese had to grab it.

"Now everyone has to hide and don't move until Old Fox reaches the center of the yard; then jump in and do your worst," Ghaz said.

Old Fox waited until it was too late, then crawled up the hill and climbed the farm. He listened and, hearing no sound, stabbed him. I was reaching for a fat goose that all the animals started working on. The dog barked, the pig screamed, the donkey was beaten, the cow moaned, the geese squeezed, the rooster sang and the pug, true to its word, knocked on Old Fox, fearful of the horror she had forgotten, jumped. He ran to meet Jack with his sharp claws. Then he took his fastest speed and passed by, crossed the hill and walked, never to be seen near that farm again.

He told some of his friends that the most terrifying animal lives there and that he has eaten all the chickens and geese and is big enough to eat them because he has at least six meters, and forks, and heads of all sizes.

Dinah Cat And The Witch

One day there was a girl named Betty. She was an orphan and a bad landlord threw her out of the house. Her only friend was a black cat named Dinah. Concrete was crying as she walked down the road and Dinah, the cat, ran to her side, rubbing against her legs. Suddenly, Betty stood in front of her hind legs. She said: "Don't cry, lover." "I'll take care of you".

Betty was so surprised to hear Dinah, the cat, talk, she cried suddenly. She said: "Poor diner, what can you do? We have to go to the city, and if I can find a job, we can live; otherwise, you have to take care of yourself because you can eat rats avoid hunger."

The cat replied: "Come with me, lover, and you will no longer need to work and starve yourself." And she put out her paw for Betty to take and walked alongside her. When they came to a path leading into the wood, Dinah Cat led Betty along this path until they were in front of two very large trees which had grown together, but there was a big opening in the trunk. "We'll go in here," said Dinah Cat, and as they stepped through, they were in a hall. She led Betty up the stairs to a room where there was a snowy-white bed and pretty furnishings. "Dinner will be served as soon as you are dressed, mistress," said Dinah Cat.

After she had gone Betty looked around, and in the closet she found pretty dresses which just fitted her. She put on one of them, and in a few minutes, she was ready for dinner. It was only then that she heard a noise of scratches at the door, and when she opened it, Dina's cat walked.

"How do you like your new home, lover?" She asked.

"Too much," Betty replied. "But we can't live in such a good home. We have no money, and, besides that, this house must belong to someone. And this dress I have on must belong to some little girl. I should not wear it."

"The dress did belong to a little girl," said Dinah Cat, "but she cannot wear it now, and she wants you to have it. And do not fret about the house. It belongs to me. I cannot tell you any more just now, but you need not worry any more about anything, for you are to live here, if you wish, after you have dinner, for then you will meet a boy, and you may not like him."

Dina took Betty's cat to a room for three, and when they were seated, a boy of Betty's age came and sat with them. He wore his hat and a thick veil was hung on it.

"I'm sorry I can't take off my hat," he said in a very sweet voice. And if you prefer, I go.

"Oh no," Betty said. "I am very grateful for allowing myself to stay and help get things done."

"You don't need to work," the boy said. "If you stay, we will be very happy."

Betty never saw his face; he lifted the veil very carefully. And there Dinah's cat sat like a lady with her knife and fork. Betty smiled to herself as she thought about eating a flying saucer.

Suddenly, Dinah the cat got up from her chair and crawled under her, and the boy shivered after shaking her chair. Betty looked around to find out why she was behaving strangely, and saw an old woman standing with a cane in her hand. He crouched where Dena was sitting, raising his cane. Betty thought she was going to hit him.

"Don't hurt Dina's cat!" He screamed, running towards the old wizard, so surprised that he let go of the cane, and Betty picked it up.

"Don't let her have it again," said the boy, "that is the cause of all our trouble."

Betty threw the stuff in a closet and locked the door. All this time the witch was stepping backward toward the door by which she entered, and she grew smaller with each step. By the time she was out of the house she looked like a black speck, and a breeze blowing just then carried her out of sight. "But how shall we ever be ourselves again?" said the boy. "She has gone, and here we are, in this state."

"Perhaps the stick will do it," said Dinah Cat.

Betty wonders what it means and the boy tells her that before the witch turned her into a cat, Dinah was her sister's cat and made her face so hateful that she had to wear a veil and they were very happy together. They have lived "But one day the old wizard came and wanted to live with us and we allowed him for a while, but he was very cross and made us so unhappy we told her that she must go away. Then she brought all this change upon us, and every once in a while, she returns and frightens us, for we do not know what she will change us into next."

"Let me get the stick," said Betty. "Perhaps we can change Dinah Cat to your sister again."

Betty opened the door of the closet, and instead of the stick there was a bright streak of light, and walking on it was a little Fairy who held a wand in her hand.

"You will soon be happy again," she told them. "I have destroyed the stick and the old witch will never return."

Then she walked over to Dinah Cat and touched her with her wand and there stood a little girl about Betty's age in place of the black cat.

"Now close your eyes," said the Fairy, "for I want the boy to remove his veil, and his face is not pleasant to look upon."

Betty did as the Fairy told her, but I am sorry to tell you that she peeked a very little. Betty closed her eyes tight after the first glimpse and waited for the Fairy to tell her to open them again, and when she did there stood the boy with a very smiling face. His sister ran to him and put her arms around him. "Now we shall be happy," she said, "and Betty will live with us. How can we thank you?" she asked the Fairy.

"Oh, I shall be repaid by seeing you all happy," the Fairy replied. "And now I must go."

"Will we see you again?" asked Betty.

"No," answered the Fairy. "I only appear when people are in trouble, and you will never need me again."

The Star and The Lily

Once there bloomed in a garden a beautiful white lily, on a long stalk so tall that she towered over all the flowers that bloomed near her.

Of course, the sunflowers at the back of the garden were much taller and the hollyhocks that grew in front of the sunflowers were taller, too, and also the sweet peas. But they were not near the beautiful lily. Beside her bloomed pansies and poppies, and many other beautiful flowers, but they were not so tall as the lily.

A rose-bush growing near the lily noticed that she drooped and did not look as happy as usual one morning, and she asked what had happened.

"Oh, I am thinking of someone I love," answered the lily, with a sigh.

"That should not bring a sigh or make you look sad, my fair friend," said the rose. "Love should make you happier than anything else in the world."

"Yes, I suppose it should," answered the lily, "but my love is so far away I am not sure that I am loved in return."

"Oh, immodest lily!" said the rose. "I thought you the most modest of all of us, and here you are in love with someone you do not know. Tell me about it, do?" said the rose, alert with interest.

"I will tell you, dear rose," said the lily, "and perhaps you can tell me how to win the love of my beloved, or how I can overcome my great love for him."

"I will do anything I can for you, my dear," said the rose, "but do tell me quick all about your love-story."

"One night," began the lily, "when everything was quiet in the garden and all the other flowers were fast asleep, I happened to raise my head and open my petals. The moonlight flowed in the garden and I was looking at all the sleeping flowers around me and I know how I woke up at that time, when I was looking at the moon in all its splendor, I saw a beautiful star looking at me slowly.

"At first, I thought it was looking at the whole garden, but then I knew all the others were asleep and I must be the one it was smiling at, for it twinkled and brightened as I gazed at it.

"I lowered my head and slyly looked again, and still the star was looking, and every time it saw me raise my head it would twinkle a smile at me. The next night I wanted to make sure it was I that the star really smiled at, and when it was bedtime, I only bowed my head and did not sleep.

"Then when the garden was still and I was sure you all slept I again raised my head and saw my star smiling straight down at me.

"This time I was sure I was the only one that the star could be smiling at, and I raised my head and opened my petals and let all the perfume of my heart go up to him, and I did not feel that I was bold, for we were all alone and he smiled down upon me, his love for two nights.

"But now I am sorrowful, for it is day and I cannot see my beloved. He seems only to show his love for me at night. What shall I do, dear rose? I am not strong enough to stay awake all day and all night too. Soon I will die if I do, and yet I cannot live if I do not see my star each night. That is why I sigh and look so sad, for I might sleep all night some time and my star will think I do not love him."

The rose shook her head. "I cannot advise you, my friend," she said; "you are in love with someone far above you, and are not even sure you are loved in return. Be wise and sleep through the night as the rest of us do, and give up this uncertain lover."

But the lily only drooped her head and sighed, and that night looked for her lover again, but the sky was dark and no bright smile greeted the poor lily. All night she gazed into the dark sky, and when the first light of day came, she was still looking for her lover.

The rose looked at her when the sun came upon them that morning, but the lily did not raise her head; she was too full of sorrow to lift her face to the sun, and by and by the rose saw that she was drooping lower and lower, so she spoke to her.

"Lily," she said, leaning closer to her, "raise your head and let the sun cheer you. You will die if you do not open your petals and get the light and air."

But the poor lily was past caring for sun or air; her petals were limp and her stalk withered.

The rose leaned closer to her as she faintly answered, and this is what she heard:

"Good-by, my friend; I shall bloom no more. My bright star hid his face from me last night and I have no desire to live longer. Perhaps I may see him after I am gone from here, and if that is true, I shall be happy, but I cannot live here and not see his face.'"

The wind blew through the garden just then and took the lily from her stem, scattering her petals far out of the garden.

"Poor lily!" murmured the rose, "she went the way we all will go, but her heart was broken and she died before her time. If she had only looked for love here in the garden instead of looking so far above her, she might be blooming now, poor lily."

Lazy Gray

All the other squirrels called him Lazy Gray, which in fact was not a very good squirrel name, but it is appropriate for this squirrel, and I want to say how he was called with such an inappropriate name.

When Lazy Gray was born, there were three little squirrels in his family, but he was the youngest and his mother thought he was the most beautiful, and the rest of the family had been expecting him long before, and his mother didn't want him to run away or to climb. To trees or any other difficult task that most squirrels have to do. And Lazy took the kindness of her mother and her brothers and sisters and asked them to attend the company. When he was thirsty and asked for a drink of water, he called his mother and said, "I am thirsty", and he briefly went down to the river, filling it with fresh, pleasant water and drinking it. And sometimes he wouldn't even say "Thank you" when he had finished.

And he used to make his brothers go on long journeys through the woods to get a particular kind of nut of which he was very fond; and if they happened to bring him one that was not good he would find fault with them and tell them that they did not know good nuts from bad ones.

All through the summer he fooled away his time sleeping and lying in the sun and never a single nut did he gather for himself. But when fall came and his two brothers were taken ill, his mother said that he would have to help her gather nuts because she could not gather enough to last the whole family through all the long winter. Lazy thought it was very hard that he should be called upon to work for his brothers even if they were sick, and he complained very bitterly about how hard it was for him to climb trees all day and store nuts. Whenever he could he stole away and lay down behind a rock and kept hidden until his mother came and found him. And then she would tell how, when it got cold and there was snow all over the ground and he was hungry, he would wish that he had been a good squirrel and had gathered the nuts while he could.

But he did not believe her and said, "Oh, I have gathered all the nuts I shall want and I am not going to work anymore," and then he would go to sleep again.

Weeks passed by, and it grew colder and colder and the snow came, and all the squirrels began to draw on their stores of nuts. Lazy found that he got pretty hungry sometimes and that the habit of eating and drinking all he wanted in the summer made him want to eat and drink all he wanted in the winter. And as he had never taught himself self-denial, he ate all he wanted, and very early in the winter he began to see that the nuts he had gathered would not last him half-way through the winter, and almost before he knew it his whole store was exhausted and he had nothing to eat.

Then he asked his mother to let him have some of the nuts that she had gathered, and being a kind mother, she let him have just as many as she could, but she still had to keep some for his sick brothers. When he wasn't giving her everything, she thought she should decide to go to the neighboring tree and ask for some of her nuts, and beg for nuts for weeks, until every squirrel in the forest hates him. She went to see him, because they knew she was begging for food to gather for himself.

At last he became so much of a nuisance that all the squirrels in the wood held a meeting and decided that each one of them would give two nuts to "Lazy," as they now all called him, and that he would have to live for the rest of the winter on the store they contributed or else starve.

When Lazy saw what a small store of nuts he would have to live upon until spring he was frightened, for he had eaten almost as many nuts as there were there in a week.

But he knew he had to make them last, so he ate very sparingly, and his sides began to be less plump and his cheeks less full, and by springtime he was a pretty sorry-looking squirrel, with his ribs showing plainly through his sides and his bushy tail looking bigger than the whole of the rest of him.

But it taught him a good lesson, and early in the next summer, just as soon as there were any nuts to be had, he began to store them away, and when winter came again, he had a big hole in the tree filled full and his mother was much pleased.

"You see," she told him, "how wicked it is not to provide for the future and store up things that are necessary against the time when you will need them."

And Lazy agreed with her and told her that never again so long as he lived would he merit the name of "Lazy."

The Old Gray Hen

"Oh baby!" Old Gray Hen said: "What a life it is! In the morning, when the day breaks in response to the call of that cow's cock, scrape all fronts for worms, sit in a nest and lay a beautiful egg there, then half an hour later, someone comes and picks up the eggs and I never see them again. Then, every spring I put a lot of eggs that I had never seen before and I'm going to sit there to feed the chickens. And then, for weeks, I have to fight for them and for myself. I don't see anything in this kind of life and I suggest changing it to fit me and most of us. The life of such a good as I am."

Gander's old father happened just when Gary Ash finished his talk. "What do you have this morning?" I asked him: "Why is everything so stained and scattered? One thinks that all the stores have turned over and all the corn has fallen to the sky."

"There is enough problem," said Gary Henry. "What do we have to live for? Something has got to be done, and, if no one else will do it, why, I shall. Things are going to be different with me."

"I guess I'll keep on as I am," said old Daddy Gander as he waddled away. "I might make them worse than they are, and they are not so bad, anyway."

"Good morning, Gray Hen," said Madam Duck. "What a fine day we are going to have! The water will be nice and warm for my ducklings, and I can give them a good swim in the pond."

"It is neither a good morning nor is it going to be a fine day, and as for swimming in the pond, if I had to mother a lot of children with as homely feet as your brood has I would want to keep them in the water all the time so that no one would see them."

"What does hennaista mean?" She said Ms. Duck deals with pirates from Turkey when she goes to the pond. "I tried to please her and she insulted me and spoke so disrespectfully to my children that I felt it was very difficult to cry."

"I almost wish I was a little anesthetized, because I've never cried a duck and I think it could be almost an eye. Maybe Gary Hunter needs good advice, and I'm going to walk. See you soon."

But the old thief saved the problem because, in a matter of minutes, Gary saw Henry go on his way. When he approached him, he said: "What a bad morning this morning, Miss Hannah; my feathers will not eat any of them directly, and every worm I have tried for breakfast has been bitter."

"You're absolutely right," said Gary Henry. "Like every recent morning, it is annoying and unpleasant, and there seems to be no promise of improvement."

"You're absolutely right," said Chabali. "I don't understand what roses and ducks are seeing right now, and I don't know about the future, why I should wait longer than the past."

"I have always felt, Mr. Gabler, that you never take half of your deserts in this warehouse. Everyone seems to think that the rooster, because it says every morning at dusk, the wisest bird is the yard, but in my in any case, I have always held you in high esteem and, often, I have talked about the nobility in your opinion and the ordinary way in which you walk there. If I had any voice in the matter, I should suggest that you be recognized as superior to the rooster. But, you see, the hens have nothing to say, although some day I feel sure that it will be different."

"You are very kind," said the gobbler, "and I feel as you do, while I have no wish to be ruler of the yard, that the hens should have more to say. You should at least have independence and do as you like."

"Oh, I have determined on that already," said Gray Hen, and she told him how she had decided to lay no more eggs and to scratch as little as she had to.

"Well," said the gobbler, "I must be off and see that none of those turkey hens get so far into the wood that they cannot find their way back again. I certainly gave the kind of advice she wanted," he said, when he had got out of her hearing, "and that was easier than getting into an argument. And, besides that, discontented people and animals are always so much more comfortable if they think others are just as unhappy as they are."

However, Old Gray Hen was good at what he said. He kept spawning and barely mentioned the amount of sand that had been scratched. He stabbed the young chicken worms that were too polite to punish the old chicken and, in general, became a public nuisance for the rest of the cattle.

They could not protect themselves, but Farmer Johnson, walking through the yard one day, noticed that the Old Gray Hen's toes had grown to a most unusual length. "I guess she doesn't do much scratching," he said as he passed along, "and I suspect she doesn't lay many eggs. I must ask mother about it when I get back to the house."

When I asked, Johnson's mother said, "No, I haven't found eggs for a month or more in Gary's nest." "So winter is not going," said farmer Johnson. "We ate it better." And the following Sunday, when Farmer Johnson had dinner, they brought a large plate of steaming fricasé to the table, and that was the end of Old Gray Hen.

A day or two later, when the thief met Mrs. Duck, she said: "I heard Gary Han left us."

"Yes," said the gobbler, "and I hope she is happier than she was here, but her contentment was greatest when others were distressed."

The Worsted Doll

Munster's good mother and his wife Jacob had five daughters. Of course, they loved them very much, but often wanted to have a child.

"So, you can help me at the store," said Jacob, a puppet maker. I added: "It's not that I would exchange one of my daughters for a boy, but I wish we had a son in addition to these five daughters."

Whether the stork heard this talk between Jacob and his wife and took offense because they questioned his judgment, or whether he thought Jacob and his wife had their number of children, I do not know, but he never called again at their door and their daughters grew up to womanhood without a brother.

One day Jacob hurried in from his shop, which was back of his house. He was very much excited, and talked so fast that good Mother Munster could not understand half he said.

"They want worsted dolls," he explained at last, "two dozen worsted dolls to be sent across the water in time for Christmas."

Jacob raised his hands with a gesture of despair, for at his shop they did not make worsted dolls, and he could not understand why anyone should want them.

"There is plenty of time to make them," Mother Munster said. "The girls and I can knit them, and we will make half of them girls and half of them boy dolls." And so, the knitted dolls were begun by good Mother Munster and her daughters.

One day, when Münster's mother tied the last doll, which was a child, she began to think that when they finished, they would lose them and send them to the other side of the sea.

He added: "I will make you very big, and if I could talk to you so you can talk and the legs you can run, and if you like a live boy you have."

Münster's mother knitted as she thought, and although she didn't know it, she tied all her dreams to the doll's body, so that when she finished, she would do what she wanted.

But he was a wise little man and would not betray him for fear of being passed on to other dolls.

It was a long journey to the other side of the ocean, and the boy doll thought it never would end. But by and by he was taken from the big packing-case and with other dolls placed in a window of a big shop.

"I wish someone would speak to me," thought the boy doll, but not a word did the other dolls utter, and as he did not wish to appear forward he kept silent also.

One day, a lady came to the store and took the doll's son with her, and one night she laid her down in a bright tin tree.

A girl entered the room after a while and when she saw the boy, she shouted: "Oh, I hope the doll is for me!"

The doll thought: "So I'm sure you'll talk to me."

And, sure enough he was given to the little girl. "I am so glad you were for me," she told him, "for I do need a father for my doll family." "Dear me," thought Boy Doll, "what a responsibility to be forced upon me so suddenly!" And not a word could he speak in reply to the little girl, because he was so surprised.

The little girl took him into a large room, which was the home of her doll family.

"This is your husband, Rosamond," she said to a large French doll, "and his name is Theodore. And this is your father," she told a group of small dolls; "he has come to live with you.

"I hope you will be a good father to them," she said to Theodore. But Boy Doll was so overcome that his tongue clung to the roof of his mouth and he was silent.

Theodore, as we may call him now, was placed in a large armchair, and the little girl left him with his family.

His noble wife raised her head and looked at Theodore's humiliation, because she was not happy to have a broken doll for her husband, and the children looked at their new father following their mother's example. And ridiculous.

"Oh, why did I leave the good mother Münster?" Theodore thought.

"She wanted a son and she would have loved me."

He sat very still for a while. He was thinking what he should do; he knew that as the father of a family he should be respected, and here were his children laughing at him.

If it were not for the haughty French wife, he might exert his authority, but Theodore was a little afraid of her.

"I'll begin with the children," he said at last, "and that may impress Rosamond."

So, while the children were giggling and whispering Theodore suddenly jumped up from his chair.

Of course, he was very stiff in his movements, as he did not have any joints, and the children laughed out and said, "Our father hasn't any joints in his legs."

A close look at Theodore's face soon calmed them, and when they reached him, they were quite scared. Theodore cleared his throat and left his hands behind.

"It's very obvious that you need a father because your behavior is terribly bad," he said. "What is your name?" He asked, combing one of them.

"Ita," he replied.

"And yours?" He pointed to another.

"May" was the answer.

"And yours, and yours, and yours, and yours, and yours and yours?" He asked him to get the names of Sally, Tomorrow, Mood, Cora, Dora and Ida.

"I divide you into two groups of four," he said. "One will be the Etta-May-Sally-Freda group and the other will be the Maude-Cora-Dora-Ida group." Called

"Yes, father," he replied all at once.

"If I always hear you tremble as I did, I will be severely punished. "

The trembling dolls replied: "Yes, sir."

"The Maudecoradoraida," Theodore said out loud.

"Yes, father," replied the second group.

"If you go back to the way I came to this house for the first time, you will be punished in the way you will remember."

The four dolls replied: "Yes, sir."

Theodore departed and walked with all the dignity he could towards his wife.

Today, the head was not long enough, because his wife's attitude towards children had shown him that he intended to become a teacher at home.

"When do we dine?" he asked.

"We have no regular hour," she answered.

"We will dine at seven," said Theodore; "breakfast at eight; the hour for lunch you may please yourself about, as I shall not be here. The children will not dine with us," he added. "And now I should like to see my room."

Rosamond, who was as completely subdued as the children, very meekly did as she was told, and Theodore found himself master without any further trouble.

But he could not forget good Mother Munster, and while he knew he should be content in the bosom of his family, he found his thoughts often with Mother Munster, across the water.

It was not an easy matter being the father of a family. If he felt like jumping or lying on the floor, there were the children, and he must not lose his dignity for a moment. "I would rather be a son," he said, "than be the father of a family. If I could get back to Germany and good Mother Munster, I should be quite happy."

Of course, this was not the proper feeling for a husband and father to have, but you must remember that Theodore had all this thrust upon him before he had any of the joys of boyhood.

One day he heard the family where he lived talking about going abroad, and saw the big trunks being packed.

Theodore thought, "Oh dear, I wonder if they would take me with them. Maybe they will go to Germany, where the good mother of Munster lives."

And then Theodore thought a very evil thought. "I enter one of the trunks and go into hiding," he said. And if I can find the Germans where Münster's mother lives, I'll never go back to be a family father, but I'll stay with Münster's mom. "And be your little boy."

Of course that was deserting his family, but Theodore did not know anything about how wrong that was, and so one day when he was left alone in the room with the trunks he climbed over the side of one of them and hid himself between the folds of a dress, without saying good-by to his wife or children.

Theodore did not feel safe until the men came for the trunks, and then his heart leaped for joy. After a long time, the trunks were opened in a hotel, and Theodore wondered what they would say when they found him.

"Here is Theodore," said the mother to her little girl, when she found him inside her dresses. "I wonder how he got in my trunk."

The little girl had not brought any of her dolls and she was so pleased to see Theodore that she hugged him.

Theodore felt guilty for doing what he wanted to do, but his love for Münster's mother was deeper than his family.

After a few weeks of visiting different places, Theodore had almost lost hope of seeing Münster's mother again, when one day they learned that "tomorrow we will go to Berlin."

Theodore repeated: "Berlin, Berlin." "Where have I heard that name before?" Then, suddenly, he arrived in Germany, where there was not much town where Münster's mother lived.

I could barely avoid jumping for joy.

One morning, when they were in Berlin for a week, the girl's father said: "Today we go to a small town to make dolls."

"I'll take Theodore, because I want to catch the doll like him," said the girl.

They got on the train completely, and then in a carriage, and stopped at a house that raised Theodore's heart so loud that he feared the fear of hearing it, because he was afraid to hear the news, by the house of Münster's mother's house. He was fine and there was his dear old lady.

They entered the kitchen and placed Theodore's girlfriend in the chest of the room.

In the thrill of seeing the doll, he forgot to take it with her and as soon as Theodore found himself alone, he rose from his chest and hid behind him.

When the girl returned from the store, she had a big doll in her arms and completely forgot Theodore.

A few days after Munster's mother cleaned her kitchen, she moved her chest, where Theodore was attracted to him.

Munster's mother picked her up. "Why, this is my son!" Said. "How did you get here?" She asked. Then he thought of the girl. He said: "I hope he doesn't send you" and held Theodore in his arms.

"Me too," said Theodore, and although he didn't speak loudly, Munster's mother seemed to understand.

"You prefer to live here, don't you?" She asked. "I'll put you in this chair in the corner and you'll be my little boy. All the girls have gone home and Jacob or I are very alone.

He said, "Look, Jacob," when he entered, he said: "Here is a broken doll I made to send water. He came back to live with us, and then we have a son."

Jacob smiled. He didn't think about the worst dolls, but he took Theodore with one hand. "You have come a long way, son," he said, "since you went here, and you can tell Monster and me everything you saw, because we were on fire three long winter nights." We are sitting "And then Theodore found a mother and a father and lived a happy and peaceful life that was not attended by the family.

But sometimes he wakes up to the sound of "Ettamaysallyfreda" or "Maudecoradoraida". And when he realizes it's just a dream, he turns around and goes back to sleep with a smile on his face that easily says "Theodore, you're a lucky man."

The Good Sea Monster

An island monster lived on an island facing the cliffs outside the ocean. He had a big head and when he opened his mouth it looked like a cave.

It was said that he was so big that he could swallow the ship and sit on the rocks on stormy nights and his eyes could sparkle for miles.

The sailors spoke with fear and trembling, but, as you can see, the sea monster was very kind to them and winked at them, showing them the stone in the storm. But as he seemed so lazy, everyone who saw him thought he must be a cruel monster.

One terrible storm occurred one night, and the monster went out to the ocean to see if any ship had crashed at night or to help someone on board if possible.

He found a little boy floating on a board. His name was Ko-Ko and he was scared when he saw the monster, but when he saw that the monster was not trying to harm him, he climbed up behind the monster and took him to a rocky island. Then the monster returned to the sea, wondering if he would be alone. But after a while the monster returned and opened its mouth wide.

Ko-Ko ran when he saw a big mouth, because he thought the monster was going to devour him, but since he didn't follow him, he came back.

The monster opened its mouth again and asked: "Do you want me to enter?" And the monster shook his head.

"This should be in my favor," Ko-Ko said, "because he could easily swallow me if he wanted to, without waiting for me to go that way."

Then Ko-Ko entered the big mouth and went down a dark hall, but what the monster wanted to do was not be able to think. Now he could see very weakly, and after a while he saw a stove, a chair and a table. "I take these out, because I'm sure I can use them," Ko-Ko said.

He took them to a cave on the island and disappeared when the monster returned. But soon he returned and opened his mouth again.

Ko-Ko walked unexpectedly and found the boxes and barrels of food he had stored in the cave. When Ko-Ko eliminated everything, the monster lay down and fell asleep.

Ko-Ko cooked his dinner and then woke up the monster and said: "Dinner is ready," but the monster shook its head and launched itself into the ocean. Soon he returned with his mouth full of fish. Then Ko-Ko knew that the monster had brought everything from the sunken ship, and wished that the monster could speak because he was no longer afraid of him.

"I wish you could talk," he said.

"I can," Hugh replied. "Nobody has ever wanted to. An old wizard turned me into a monster and put me on an island where no one could reach me and the only way I can go back to my original way is for some to wish."

"I wish," said Ko-Ko.

"You had your wish, and I can talk, but to be a man I have to wish someone else," said the monster.

The monsters and Ko-Ko lived on the island for a long time. He rode Ko-Ko on his back for a long time, and when the waves were too high, Ko-Ko feared the monster would open his mouth and Ko-Ko would enter and return safely to the island.

One night, after the storm, Ko-Ko saw something floating in the water, and he jumped on the monster's back and swam towards him.

It turned out to be a little girl, about San Ko-Ko, who had been aboard a shipwreck, and was taken to the island.

At first, he was afraid of the monsters, but when he discovered that he had rescued Ko-Ko and him and brought them all his food, he was equally interested in him.

"I wish it was a man," he said one day, while sitting with Ko-Ko on his back, preparing to sail. The splash brought both children to the water, and there was an old man instead of a monster. I took the children in his arms and brought them to the beach.

"But now that you're a man, what will we do for the food?" Ko-Ko asked.

"We don't want anything for now," replied the old man. "I am a god of the sea and I can do many things now that I am fit. We will transform the island into a beautiful garden and have a castle when your daughter and son are raised and married, and all the gods of the sea and the nymphs will take care of you.

"I will get you out of the ocean on the back of my dolphins."

Ko-Ko and the girl lived on the enchanted island, and everything that the Old God of the Sea had promised came true.

Mother Turkey and Her Chicks

The Turkish mother believed in the old custom that her grandmother had taught her: "The first bird kills the worm" and that the sun sets each night, its chickens climbing the highest branch that could climb an old apple tree. Reach, catch and sing. Sleep with this lullaby:

"Close your eyes, my little turkey.

Hide your head, don't look.

Mother knows swamp fox tricks,

And he will watch while sleeping. "

The Turkish mother had told them about the swamp fox that lived in a hole on the other side of the hill, and there is no need to mention this name to obey.

When her mother reached the end of the verse, she said, "I wish we could just look at her." "If I had known him, I wouldn't have known him."

His mother replied, "Oh, yes, you will." It has very long tail and nose and sharp teeth! Oh dear! "He was screaming as he thought about his wings.

"If he comes at night, will you wake us up?" Another girl asked.

"I don't need it," the Turkish mother said. "He listens to us. He's a very polite and always polite person, and he says good things. But he covers his head, it's too late."

"Close your eyes, my little turkey.

Hide your head, don't look.

Mother knows swamp fox tricks,

And he will watch while sleeping. "

When the Turkish mother reached the end of the verse, this time all the girls were asleep.

The Turkish mother spread her wings once or twice and turned her head in all directions and then prepared for a nap.

The moon woke up and shone, not far from what a big black dog looked like, walking cautiously toward the tree. The Turkish mother looked at the other and saw the tail of the bush and looked harder at her limbs to see if her children were safe there, as she knew that the weaver's fox had reached one of her chickens. Come back if I could.

"Good evening, the fox came close enough to hear me," the fox said. "I was sure I knew your brilliant face; you would surely make the most exciting picture in the moonlight. "

Mr. Fox was somewhat surprised by this compliment, and liked it because he was usually the one talking and listening to the turkey, not daring to move and talk.

Surprisingly, he recovered from being under the tree and said, "You are the most ridiculous lover of Turkey and I can only return that interpretation by saying that you are in the moonlight." But if you enjoy this beautiful night, you must step out of the tree and walk the hill. "

"She certainly is right, but I can't think of leaving my children alone," Ms. Turkey replied. "I have to be very happy about taking care of the little kids, and if you leave them with me, I'm going to tell you a story that I'm sure I will love whenever you like," said Mr. Fox. I know you will be interested.

At this moment, the turkey chicks woke up and listened to what the fox said. She seemed so kind and polite that they had completely forgotten to stop being scared, and when she told them a story, one of them said, "Oh, please, mother, and let her have an affair. We'll be great if you want to be good."

The fox said: "You see, dear lady," the little ones are willing to stay with me. Go and enjoy the moonlight. "

The Turkish mother looked at her children in a way that told them bluntly: "Shut up," and then said to Mr. Fox: "I appreciate your kind offer, and if my children were good, they should have been very happy to be with them. But they are sick and so thin that I have to be very careful that they sleep and eat, or they will not get fat on the next Thanksgiving, and that can be a shame. "

When the fox heard this, he wasn't anxious enough for the chicks to fall, so he said: "I know how anxious you are, Turkish lover, and if you come there, I can talk to you without hearing it. It will tell you what to give them fat ".

"If she can't catch the chicks, she'll catch me," Turk said. "But I am a bird to be caught even by this evil co-worker."

Ms. Turkey did not respond to these final statements. He was thinking about the trap his teacher had set the day before. He said: "I wish I had walked a little so that my children could see what a great tail and shrub you are." "They have never seen your handsome neighbor."

Mr. Fox was very proud of his tail, so he came out of the shade of the tree.

"Tell her how beautiful she is," Turkey's mother told her chickens.

"Oh, he's not handsome!" One said, and the other said: "I wish we had that tail instead of these straight feathers." "You are the most beautiful creature I have ever seen in my life, and I have seen many in my time," said Mrs. Turkey.

At this time, the fox was so happy that he was ready to do anything to show his charms, so when the Turkish lady said, "I wish you could run away and show them how you can run and jump," he asked as he could jump to show his tenacity.

"The top of that pig's head would be a good place," said the turkey, saying he knew he had no head and was almost full of water.

Mr. Fox ran and splashed and entered the earthquake. He tried to leave, but it was in vain. The bag was too big, and then the farmer came out listening to the noise and finished with Mr. Fox soon.

The little turkeys were awake and trembling with their mother, but when the farmer went home, he began to sing:

"Close your eyes, my little turkey.

Hide your head, don't look.

Mother knows swamp fox tricks,

And he will watch while he sleeps. "

And in a matter of minutes everyone was silent again in the courtyard.

Tearful

One day there was a girl named Tearful because she often cried.

If she couldn't get her way, she would cry. If I couldn't have everything I wanted, I would cry.

One day her mother told her she would cry if she cried. "You're like a baby crying to the moon," she said, and she wouldn't be happy if she gave it to her because the moon could be suitable for anyone outside its potential use. And this is your way; if you get half of what you cry for, it's not in your favor. "

Tears could not be heard or heard by her mother's wise words, and the same cry continued.

One morning she was crying while going to school because she wanted to stay home when she noticed a frog next to her.

"Why are you looking at me?" she asked.

The frog said in response, "Because soon you will create a pool around you with your tears. I always wanted the pool for me."

"I will not make any ponds for you," said Tears. And I don't want to follow you. "

The frog continued on its pelvis, crying and running, but the frog tied faster and couldn't run, so he started crying again.

"Come on the terrible green frog!" said

Finally, I was so tired of sitting on the road by the cliffs and crying all the time.

The frog replied, "Now, I'll have my pond soon."

Tears were crying louder than ever, she couldn't see, her tears fell too fast and she heard a loud cry. He opened his eyes and saw the water around him.

I was on a small island in the middle of the pond. The frog came out of the pond and made a terrific make-up while sitting by it.

"I hope you are happy," Tears says. "You have your own dock, why not stay there?"

"Wings!" The frog replied, "I wish I could not use it now. Your tears are my salt and my pool is all I have. If only your tears were fresh, I would I was lucky. "

"If you don't like to stay, you don't need to stay. You don't need to blame my tears," Tear said.

"Stop! Stop!" The frog cried and he was excited. If you cry, you will flood.

The tears saw the water running around him, so he stopped for a minute. "what can I do?" "I can't swim and die if I have to stay here," he asked. And then he started crying again.

The frog jumped up and down in front of her, shaking his front legs and telling her to hurry. "If you were only crying," he said, "maybe I can help you, but if you cover your salt tears, I can't do anything."

Tearful, she listened and promised not to cry if she drove her away from the island.

"There is only one way to know," said the frog. "You have to smile; this pool dries up and we can escape."

"But I don't feel like smiling and crying again," said Tears.

"Watch out!" The frog said: "If you cry again, you will surely cry."

The tear began to laugh. "It won't be too scary, will I sink in my tears?"

The frog said: "That's right, smile." "The pond is smaller than before." And he stood on his hind legs and began to dance with joy.

The tears laughed again. "Oh, you're so funny!" Said. "I wish I had your picture. I've never seen a frog dance before."

"You have a rock under your arm," said the frog. "Why don't you take a picture?" The frog grabbed a stick and hit it to the ground, then leaned against it with one arm or front foot and stood up, crossing its legs.

The tear attracted her to that position, and then lifted her up as if she were dancing, and tried to get him out of the way, but the resemblance was not very good.

"You like?" He asked the frog while holding the rock to see it. I was so surprised that the tear laughed again. "You don't think you're handsome, right?" She asked.

"I never thought it would look as bad as these photos," said the frog. "Let me try to paint your picture," he said.

She said: "Now stay well, when you're sitting in front of Tearful, and smile. "

The tear did his will and delivered the rock in minutes. "Where is my nose?" Laughing tears.

"Oh, I forgot my nose!" The frog said. "But don't you think your eyes are beautiful and big, and your mouth too?"

"They are certainly in the big picture," Tearful said. "I hope I'm not just like that."

"I don't think each one of us is an artist," Frog replied.

Tears sprouted around him. "Why, where is the pond?" She asked. "It is gone".

"I thought it would dry if you smiled," said the frog. "And I think we have both learned a lesson. I never want to have a group of my own again. I have to be alone without my classmates, and after that, it can be salt, like this one. Certainly, never cry for the little things again, because you see what happens to you and then you look much smarter. "

"Maybe yes, but your images of me make me skeptical," said Tearful, "but I'm smiling much happier and I don't want to be on an island again, even with such a nice companion of who you are."

"Look at the tears," said the frog as he turned.

Where The Sparks Go

One night, when it was windy and cold outside the house, a very good friend of the cat and the dog stood in front of the fire. The wood was drowning and exploding, causing sparks to jump. Some flew down the chimney, others were parked on the coal bed, and others flew with steam and slowly closed their eyes and fell asleep.

One of the sparks was farther from heartburn and rotted nearby. This made him jump and woke the dog.

"You almost burned your fur coat, Miss Poe," said the dog.

The cat replied: "No, really." "I'm stuck in these stupid sparks very fast."

"Why do you call them stupid?" The dog asked. "I think they look great and help us keep warm."

"Yes, it's true," said the cat, "but those who fly on a night like a chimney are certainly stupid, when they can be warm and comfortable inside; in my opinion, I can't see why they fly." "

The spark that flew near Pace was still blinking, and when he heard the cat's words, it burst slowly.

"You wouldn't call us stupid if you knew our reason," he said. "You can't see what we're doing, but if you look for the fireplace and see what would happen if we were lucky enough to go to the top, you wouldn't call us stupid."

The dogs and cats were very curious to know what had happened, but Spark told them to look for themselves. Pus was very cautious and told the dog to look first, so he bravely entered the fireplace and stuck his head out. She quickly withdrew it because she had her hair down, which made her cry and run to the other side of the room...

Mrs. Pussy smoothed her coat and was very happy to be very wise. He approached the dog and asked him to approach the fire, but he understood why the burned child was scared and at a safe distance.

Pace returned the spark and continued questioning. "We cannot enter the fire," he said. "Now, beautiful glow, tell us what you get when you get up from the fireplace. I'm sure you're soot and this can't get you to the top."

"Oh, you're so wrong," said Spark. "We are not far from the black when we escape from the top of the chimney, for the first time we reach it, we live forever in the bright sky. You can find all our brothers and sisters who were lucky and I have reached my peak almost every night. I think sometimes the wind swallows them, because there are nights when we can't shine spark effects. "

"Who told you this?" She said: "Have any of the sparks come back and told you they can live forever?"

"Wow no!" "But we can see them, right? And we said, of course, that we all want to shine forever."

"I said you're stupid, and now I know," Cat said. "It's not the sparks you see; they're stars in the sky."

"You can call them what you want, but we make the lights you see," Spark replied.

The cat said, "Well, if you follow my advice, you will be right in the chimney, once you go from top to bottom of the chimney. The stars you see flash far above the chimney, and never again. You couldn't reach them."

But the spark is not convinced. At that moment someone opened the door and blew the spark plug in the fireplace. In a matter of minutes, I was flying through the fireplace with others.

Pace watched the fire for a minute and then looked at the dog.

"Finally, the spark is right," the dog said. "Let's see if we can see it."

Busted and blinked. "Maybe that's true," he replied. "Anyway, I'll go with you and watch."

Mr. 'Possum

Mr. 'Possum lived in a tree in the forest where Mr. Burro lived, and one day before Mr. 'Possum's spring, he was very hungry.

He ran to Mr. Squirrel's house and tried to get an invitation for breakfast, but Mr. Squirrel was enough for himself. I knew that Mr. 'Possum always lived with his neighbors when he could, so he said: "Surely you had breakfast a long time ago, Mr. 'Possum, you are such an intelligent colleague, so I suggest that I will not give"

Of course, Possum said yes, and only entered the country to make calls. I was going to Mr. Rabbit's house.

But he did not see a greater success in Mr. Rabbit because he blew his nose and when he saw who was there, he said: "I am as busy as I can prepare for my spring planting. Do you come and help sort the seeds?"

Mr. Rabbit knew that the easiest way to get rid of Mr. 'Possum was to work for him.

Mr. 'Possum replied: "I am glad to help you, but I'm in a hurry this morning. I have an important issue with Mr. Bear, and I just stopped to tell him how he is doing."

"Mr. 'Possum, I'm afraid I won't have the day," Mr. Rabbit said. "The peak is too early to wake up, right?"

"I thought the sun was good and warm and it could come out, and I think it would make him happy to take me there," Possum said. "Besides, I want to see it in business."

Now Mr. 'Possum knew very well that Mr. Bear would not wake up, and he wanted to find him sleepy.

He went to the door and knocked slowly, then waited and, not hearing any movement inside, went to a window and looked. There was Mr. Bear's chair and pipe when he left them while he slept. He looked out the window of the room and saw on the bed a large pile of beds and only the smallest tip of Mr. Bear's nose.

Mr. 'Possum listened and shook a little, because Mr. Bear could breathe hard and sound like anything.

"Oh, he's been sleeping for another week!" Mr. 'Possum said. "What's the use of fear?" He walked through the house until he reached the slaughterhouse window. Then he stopped and saw.

He put his foot in the door and listened. Everyone was still, so he hit the ground. Mr. 'Possum looked around the house full of bears. He didn't know where to start, he was very hungry.

He became so interested and was so greedy that he forgot all about Mr. Bear's house and clothes, and stayed there and ate and ate.

Then he fell asleep, and the first thing he knew was a pair of bright eyes looking out the window, and a large head with a red mouth full of long white teeth rose in the cabins.

Mr. 'Possum thought his time had come, so he simply closed his eyes and pretended to be dead, but looked around to see what had happened.

He had a big head and, while in the yard, Mr. 'Possum saw Mr. Fox, and the next thing he knew was that Mr. Fox came out of the storm with an explosive sound, hit a pot of beans and then more ones. Crush the food jars.

The noise was enough to wake all the bears for miles, and Mr. 'Possum was scared to hear Mr. Bear grow up in the next room.

While Mr. Fox was on the floor trying to stand up, Mr. 'Possum jumped and came out the window like a flash. Mr. Fox saw something, but he didn't know what it was, and before he could escape, he opened the trick's door, where Mr. Bear was standing with a candle in his hand.

"Oh oh!" He growled, "So you try to steal me while I sleep," and nodded at Mr. Fox.

"Wait, wait," Mr. Fox said. "Let me explain to you, my dear bear. You are wrong; I was trying to protect your home. Now you blame me for that. You are more ungrateful. I know what to do next time."

Mr. Bear looked at him. His mouth showed no sign of food, and Mr. Fox opened his mouth and told him to look.

"I wonder who it could have been?" he said, when he was satisfied that Mr. Fox was not the thief. "It could have been that Possum partner. I will go to his house in the morning."

The next morning, Mr. Bear called Mr. 'Possum. He found him sleeping soundly, and when he finally opened the door, he was rubbing his eyes as if he wasn't half awake.

"Why, how are you?" He said, when he saw Mr. Bear. "I didn't suppose you were still awake." "You did not do it?" Mr. Bear asked, and then looked at Mr. 'Possum's coat. "What's wrong with your coat?" he asked. "You have white hair that stand out and the rest of your coat is also almost white."

Now Mr. 'Possum had a black coat before, and ran to the mirror and looked at himself. That was true, it was almost white. He knew what had happened. He was so scared when he was caught in Mr. Bear's pantry by Mr. Fox, and heard Mr. Bear growl, that he had become almost white with fear.

"I've been terribly sick," he told Mr. Bear, returning to the door. "And I've been here alone this winter. It was a terrible disease; I think that's what caused it."

Mr. Bear left, shaking his head. "That guy is cunning," he said. "I'm sure it was the thief and yet he certainly seems sick."

After that, all the possums were opaque white, with long white hair scattered here and there on their fur. They could never overcome the mark that the thief Mr. 'Possum left in his race.

The Rooster That Crowed Too Soon

Red Rooster felt it was time for him to reveal a new door that he had come to live in the warehouse, which was a very brave rooster, as well as the owner of the warehouse.

Then, the next time he saw Drake, he said: "I think you have been in many battles, and no doubt the house you just lost will lose your protection and your company."

"No," Drake replied. "I've never been in a fight. I don't fight with anyone. I think I live in peace with everyone around me."

"Oh well, that's fine for you," Rooster said. "" But for me, it's different. I have to protect the chickens and protect me too. I whip here, and nobody dares to enter my yard. "

Drake did not answer, because right after that, a strange rooster entered the courtyard and a red rooster with wide wings hit him.

He nodded to the aggressor and incited him until he was happy to escape.

"There, what did I tell you?" The red rooster said to Drake again. "I am the biggest fighter in this part of the country. I am not afraid of anything."

"Oh, don't talk too much about it," said the dog in his house. "I think there are some things you weren't even afraid of. I think you ran away from a fox," Rooster said.

"I'm not afraid of the fox," said the rooster. "I can make him scream with a terrible voice. The Master knows that when I make a lot of noise it is time for him to find the cause. Oh, I am very brave and I can take care of myself."

Red Rooster felt so brave that he thought that the highest place he could put on the wall would be a good place to talk about his courage, so he flew over the wall with a door and then to the chicken coop.

Miss Pig was on the other side of her pen. She said: "Miss Pig, have you seen me whip that reckless cock that entered our yard?"

Mrs. Pig was upset because she couldn't, since she couldn't see over the wall.

"You've surely lost a great vision," Rooster said, stretching his neck and walking on the roof. "I am a brave colleague. I will never let anyone who does not belong here come. I just told Drake New about my bravery and courage."

"If you need protection at all times, feel free to contact me," he said, as Drake said, just when the new Drake and his family had passed through the chicken coop.

Rubin, not far from his roof, turned red and the rooster fled towards him. He said: "Go away." "I'm very stubborn and brave, and if you were the size of a big cow, I should have attacked that. I'm not afraid of anything."

The red knot rose from side to side, coughing and thinking how brave he was, and acting so magnificently that he ignored the alarming screams of birds in the courtyard beneath him...

In an instant, a great hawk disappeared and held the rooster in its paw. It began to fly just when the shot rang and the rooster fell to the ground.

He jumped and shook himself and watched his teacher lift the dead hawk.

"I think the hawk won't come back here," he said. "It was a very tough fight, but I won, even if I got in trouble." "Well, if you're not a smart colleague!" The dog laughed: "But I was not the only one to see that the hawk started with you, and we all know that if Master had not shot him, you would not be here until tomorrow morning."

"No," Robin said from a tree. "You were telling me how brave you were, and the hawk was not half the size of a cow. When he approached, you were not brave. You did nothing. You will soon find a hawk a little bigger than you."

Drake and his family were listening, and Mrs. Pig lowered her head to listen to the wall. The poor red rooster felt that it was no longer time to dissipate his courage, so he left with all the dignity that could be avoided.

"I was very busy early," Drake said.

"I was too busy," said the dog.

"I was crying too loudly, or I heard warning shouts from chickens and chickens," Robin said.

The Mirror's Dream

"The idea of putting myself in the attic!" The old table said, because it expands both sheets in a gesture of despair. "I've been in the yard for fifty years in the lower hall and now they've sent me to the garbage room." And his leaves collapsed with a sigh beside him.

"I was there more than that time," said the sofa. "Many a courtship I have helped along."

"What do you think of me?" asked an old mirror that stood on the floor, leaning against the wall. "To be brought to the attic after reflecting generation after generation. All the famous beauties have looked into my face; it is a degradation from which I can never recover. This young mistress who has come here to live does not seem to understand the dignity of our position. Why, I was in the family when her husband's grandmother was a girl and she has doomed me to a dusty attic to dream out the rest of my days."

The shadows deepened in the room and gradually the discarded mirror ceased to complain. It had fallen asleep, but later the moonlight streamed in through the window and showed that its dreams were pleasant ones, for it dreamed of the old and happy days.

The door opened softly and a young girl entered. Her hair was dark and hung in curls over her white shoulders. Her dark eyes wandered over the room until she saw the old mirror.

She ran across the room and stood in front of it. She wore a ring skirt that began with her pale gray dress and fine pink pendants that began at the waist and ended at the end of her wide skirt.

The pink strips were bent over her waist and skirt, and she also used them in her dark ovens, where one of the lost flowers was bolder than her soft cheek.

She stood in front of the mirror and looked for a minute. Then she leaned down and said with a smile: "I think you will, I should talk at night."

She seemed to fade away in the moonlight, and the door opened again and a lady entered, and with her came five handsome children.

They went to the mirror, and one little girl with dark curls and pink cheeks went close and touched it with her finger. "Look," she said to the others, "I look just like the picture of mother when she was a girl." And as they stood there a gentleman appeared beside them and put his arm around the lady and the children gathered around them. They seemed to walk along the moonlight path and disappear through the window.

Softly the door opened again and an old lady entered, leaning on the arm of an old gentleman. They walked to the mirror and he put his arms around her and kissed her withered cheek.

"You are always young and fair to me," he said, and her face smiled into the depths of the old mirror.

The moonlight created a halo that faded around him.

The morning light came on in the window and the mirror was finished.

The door opened and the young woman entered the room. Her dark hair was long over her head, and her dark eyes stared at the room until they fell into a corner. She turned to her, opened it and took off a pale gray dress with pink. She put it on and then lowered the hair that had fallen on her shoulders.

She ran to the old mirror and looked at herself. "I look like my grandmother," she said. "I wear this at an old popular party at night.

Grandfather proposed to grandmother the night she wore this dress." Her cheeks turned very pink as she said this, and she ran out of the room.

Then one day the door opened again and a bride entered, leaning on the arm of her young husband. There were tears in her eyes, although she was smiling. She led him in front of the old mirror. "This old mirror," she said, "has seen all the brides in our family for generations, and I am going far away and may never look into it again. My brother's wife does not want it down-stairs, and I may be the last bride it will ever see," and she passed her hand over its frame caressingly.

And then she went away and the old mirror was left to its dreams for many years. Then one day the door opened again and a lady entered; with her was a young girl.

The lady looked around the attic room until she saw the mirror. "There it is," she said. "Come and look in it, dear." The young girl followed her. "The last time I looked into this dear old mirror," the lady said, "was the day your father and I were married. I never expected to have it for me. But your cousin wants to rebuild the house, and that's it. He doesn't want old things, and they want me to have them. "

"Oh, mother, they are beautiful!" The girl said, looking towards the room. "We will never associate with them; we will take them home and forget that they have never been discarded."

And so, the mirror and the sofa and the desk and many of the last days went to live in love with them, and the old mirror still reflects the dark-haired girls and women whose smiles are deep and their beauties they also see.

The Disorderly Girl

When her mother called her, Louise was out of the house with her sleigh. Louise hesitated because she knew her mother would call her to organize her playroom and wanted to go to the beach with other children.

She turned slowly and asked, "What, mother?"

Her mother replied: "Your playroom must be in order before you can play."

"You have had plenty of time this week to do it, but you have neglected it, and now you cannot put it off another day."

"Why can't Jane do it?" asked Louise.

"Jane will clean the room," her mother replied, "but it is your duty to pick up the books and toys that are strewn around."

Louise pouted, but she knew that she must do as her mother said, and she took off her hat and coat and went up to her play-room. She went in and closed the door.

The room was certainly a mess. The books were on the floor and the games on the table, the dolls spread throughout the room.

Louise had chosen most of the things that was going through her little friend Clara's window. "Clear!" She called: "Wait for me, I have to set up my game room to go to the beach." But Clara doesn't wait.

Louise closed the window, threw herself on the couch and began to cry, saying she thought she meant everyone to the beach except her.

Suddenly she saw two girls walking towards her. They were exactly like her dolls, Bella and Emily, only they were as big as her.

Louise tried to get up, but couldn't move.

Bella Doll told Louise as she approached: "Let's throw her out."

"Yes, and comb your hair," said Emily Doll.

Then Louise knew what had happened: she had become a doll and the dolls were little girls.

"The girls dressed Louise and dressed her in a nightgown," Louise said. Then they combed her hair and pulled it terribly.

"I don't know how she likes to fix her hair," Bella Doll said.

"She knows how it feels, now," said Emily.

"I think she better go out," said Bella Doll, "instead of going to bed," and they dressed her in a thin white dress. "Now we will take her out in the cold; that is the way she does with us."

They fastened her clothes with pins and pushed them right through her body, and after she was dressed, they changed their minds about taking her out and threw her on the floor and began playing games.

"I wonder if they are going to leave me here," thought Louise. "Someone will be sure to step on me." Just then she saw a Teddy Bear lying on his side under the couch. "Why are you under there?" Louise asked.

"The little girl who was playing with me dropped me back of the couch a week ago," he said, "and I have been here ever since, and you will probably remain on the floor where you are now, for she never picks up her toys. She is a very careless girl."

Louise didn't answer, because that's when Emily Doll found a book in the bank and kicked Louise off the floor. Bella Doll prepared a game of croquet and one of the balls hit Louis in the head. Then Emily dropped her book and said, "Come on, Bella, let's go out."

Louise watched as they left. "Oh, that's the way she always leaves her room because she couldn't see the two girls under the sofa, and she thought it was Louise who came out the door," said Teddy Bear. She never thinks of us, "or how uncomfortable we can be, because she is a very careless and reckless girl."

The door opened and Bella Doll entered. She went to the bank for her hat and saw Luiz's foot on her head. Louise shouted, "If she puts me," she would break me and cry out loud.

There she was at the bank. She has been asleep. She got up and finished her work, when suddenly she thought of the teddy bear and looked under the bench. I was there where I had dreamed.

Louis picked her up and laid her on the chair. Then she looked at Bella's dress to make sure she didn't have a pin, and after looking at Emily, she put them both in a comfortable place.

Her books were put on a shelf, and she resolved never again to let her room get so untidy or to let her dolls or Teddy Bear suffer from neglect. "Perhaps they do feel things," she said. "Anyway, I'll be sure not to hurt them or let them be in uncomfortable positions, for I was very miserable lying on the floor thinking I might be stepped upon."

The Shoemaker Rat

One day, a rat entered the piles of knives, and after eating everything he wanted, he became bolder and went to the kitchen.

There the cook saw him and chased him with a broom, but he was not been able to hit him as he ran out of the door, he picked up a pair of shoes that were standing near and threw them after him.

The rat picked them up and put them on. On his way home he met a cat. "What have you on your feet?" he asked the rat.

"Can you not see, my dear Tom?" said the rat. "They are shoes. I am a shoemaker, and, of course, must wear my own product."

"Make me a pair," said the cat, "and I will spare your life."

"Very well," replied the rat, "but first you must bring me some leather."

Then the cat escaped and returned with two skins.

When the rat saw the amount of leather, an idea occurred to him.

"My dear Tom," he said, "I can make you a suit of clothes and a pair of gloves as well as the shoes, and you will be the envy of all the other cats."

Tom was delighted and told the rat to hurry and make the outfit.

The wise rat first made the gloves and covered Tom's sharp claws. Then he made the shoes for the hind feet, and when he had that done, he felt safe.

"Now you must wait," he said; "until I get something with which I can fasten the coat." He ran away and returned with some long, sharp thorns.

Next the rat put the leather around Tom's body and drew it tight, fastening it with a thorn which he pushed so that the sharp point pricked Tom.

"What are you doing?" asked Tom, angry at being hurt; but he could not move, the leather costume was so stiff and tight, but he grabbed at the rat with his mouth, and caught him by the tail.

The rat ran, leaving his tail in Tom's mouth.

"I'll know you," Tom called after him. "When I am out of this suit, I will catch you and eat you."

The rat had not thought of that and he wondered what he should do, but he was a wise old fellow, and when he reached home, he called all his brothers and sisters and cousins and aunts about him.

"I met a cat today," he said. I had arrived in a city where all styles were new and he told me that all the rats in the city would be cut by brewing, so I had mine done. If you want to be in style," he told them, "you must have your tails like mine."

"Does it hurt?" asked one.

"Not a bit," answered the sly fellow, "and you have no idea how comfortable it is running about without a tail to look after. It is very expensive to have it cut," he explained; "that is the only difficult part. I had to pay twenty pieces of cheese. But I watched while another fellow was having his cut, and I am sure I can do it as well as the rat that did mine. And if you wish to be in style at a very low rate, I will take off your tails for five pieces of cheese each."

All rats agreed and ran for cheese, and the knife was crushed while they were lost.

Soon he had the tails cut and a goodly store of cheese. "Now," he said to himself, "Tom will never know me from the other rats."

He kept his eyes open for Tom, who had called his friends to help him out of his suit and told them to watch for a rat without a tail. But when they saw all the bored mice, they stopped looking for someone to put Tom in leather clothes, and Tom, who didn't like to hunt very well, gave up. "But the next time I meet a rat," said Tom, "I will catch him, no matter whether he has a tail or not."

The Contest

The old white rooster was dead.

The chickens were standing in groups of three, and the four corners around the yard, the turkeys gathered around the big cabin, and seemed to be talking very seriously.

The ducks stood around an old drake that shook its head as it spoke.

The geese listened to the giant very carefully, and he stretched his neck and seemed to be trying to impress them.

"I don't see any reason why I shouldn't be the king of the yard," he said. "The white rooster is dead and there is no other rooster to replace it. I'm going to see the chickens and ask them what they think."

He told them: "The white rooster is dead, and I think I have to be the king of the yard. My neck is very long and I can see all the birds above; I see no reason not to take it. The place of the white rooster."

The turkeys and geese, approaching the harbor, approached the chickens as soon as they could hear what he was saying.

The turkey thief heard the last part of the gendarme's comments: "How can you say that you can see all the heads? Have you forgotten me and my stature? And as king," said the rooster. "I am more majestic than any rooster. No, in fact, you should never think of a ruler, Sir Gander. I have to be the king of the yard. "

The man extended his hand from a distance and spread his wings, allowing them to land and play loudly.

Ducks and Drakes stood up and listened to all this talk, and while pulling Drake's knob he said: "I can't understand why anyone should think of the kingdom when one knows the world. I am the one who rules because I have been around the pond and it is huge; because of my knowledge, I think I have to be the king. "

"He must not be king," whispered an old chicken to another. "It forces us to go to the water and we all drown."

They had been talking for a long time, without making a decision, when the dog was there. "What's up?" it asked.

"The old white rooster is dead," said a moron who spoke with his family to listen to the debate. "And I think it should be the king, and Drake and the Giants think they should be, but you can certainly see that I am in a position to comply with the patio rule. "

"You can solve this very easily," said the dog. "All of you can become emperors and you will discover who is the most suitable for the government." And so, it was decided, and the hunter was the first to go to trial. Poor chicken is shown after turkeys because the thief insisted on barking in the yard. Gander and Drake will not pass, so Gander and his family walk on one side of the dandelion, and Drake and his family on the other.

The poor chicken was crying from behind. "I've never been so humiliated in my life, and that's not true," said an old chicken.

The next day, there was much dissatisfaction with the way the barbarian was surprised that the dog decided that Drake should take his turn.

"Everyone has to learn to swim," Drake said. "Come to the pond," and when he started, his family followed him.

"What did I tell you?" "This will be our end," said the old chicken.

Geese don't mind being in the water for a while, but the turkeys put so much fog and the chickens were raised so high that the dog had to decide that there was no good king.

Knowing that the time had come, the bird stretched its neck and seemed very important.

He told the chickens: "You shouldn't go to the pond, but you must learn to fly. "And as he spoke, he spread his wings and flew, and flew over the fence, the geese followed him.

The turkeys fly over the fence and roast there, but the chickens and ducks stand on the ground and look at them in the most daunting way, and say in front of the garrison, who laughed at them: "You must be scary, because you don't see all our attractions and you can never fly over this fence."

"There is a teacher," he said. "He is coming down the road and has something under his arm. I tell you what he says when he approaches."

The chickens were trying to look under the fence and through the holes.

The bracelet searched for a minute, and then said, "I think ...", then stopped. "If that's all". "This is a rooster."

The hunter flew down, followed by the turkeys, and led the giant master and his family to the courtyard. "You will glue your wings for tomorrow," he said, and then released a large yellow and black rooster under his arm, flying toward the ground, watching, flapping his wings and he was busy. "I am the rooster of this walk and the king of this courtyard."

Drake reunited his family and began working for the pool, and the geese and geese followed him.

The turkey spread its wings and held its head firmly when she left with her family. But it didn't affect the new cock. He was the ruler and he knew it.

"Now the sun knows when it will rise and we know when to wake up," said a chicken.

He said: "Yes," said another, "and we had a narrow escape; for a while it was as if our family had lost their social position, but now that we have a new king we can raise our heads again and in the case of others, if we have to go over the board to do it. "

The dog laughed as he escaped. "I always knew that the new rooster would come, but I thought it was good to know that they were good at taking care of their flock," he said.

Why The Morning-Glory Sleeps

One day the flora was given into a very angry discussion over the sun, of whom they were very fond.

"Surely you all must know that he loves me best," said the rose. "He shines upon me and makes me sweeter than any of you, and he gives me the colors that are most admired by man."

"I do not see how you can say that," said the dahlia. "You may give forth more fragrance than I can, but you cannot think for a second that you are more beautiful. Why, my colors are richer than yours and last much longer! The sun certainly loves me the best."

The modest lily looked at the dahlia and said in a low, sweet voice, "I do not wish to be bold, but I feel that the sun loves me and that I should let you know that he gives to me more fragrance than to any of you."

"Oh, oh! Hear lily!" said the others in chorus. "She thinks the king of day loves her best."

The lily hung her head and said no more, for the other flowers quite frightened her with their taunts.

"How can any of you watched you're the great loved of the solar?" stated golden glow.

"When you behold my glowing color which the sun bestows on me, do any of you look so much like him as I do? No, indeed; he loves me best."

The hollyhock looked down on the others with pitying glances. "It is plain to be seen that you have never noticed that the sun shines on me with more warmth than on you, and now I must tell you he loves me best and gives me the tenderest of his smiles. See how tall I am and how gorgeous are my colors. He loves me best."

"When it comes to sweetness, I am sure you have forgotten me," said the honeysuckle. "Why, the king of day loves me best, you may be sure! He makes me give forth more sweetness than any of you."

"You may be very sweet," said the pansy, "however certainly you know that my pet call is coronary heart's-ease and that the sun loves me first-rate.

To none of you does he give such velvet beauty as to me. I am nearest his heart and his best beloved."

The morning-glory listened to all this with envy in her heart. She did not give forth sweetness, as many of the others, neither did she possess the beauty of the rose or the pansy.

"If only I could get him to notice me," she thought. "I am dainty and frail, and I am sure he would admire me if only he could behold me; but the others are always here and in such glowing colors that poor little me is overshadowed by their beauty."

All day morning-glory idea of the sun and wondered how she ought to entice his attention to herself, and at night she smiled, for she had thought of a plan.

She would get up early in the morning and greet him before the other flowers were awake.

She went to mattress early that night time in order that she may not oversleep inside the morning, and while the primary streak of sunrise showed inside the sky morning-glory opened her eyes and shook out her delicate folds. The dew turned into on her and she grew to become her face toward the sun.

As soon as she peeped into the garden the sun beheld her. "How dainty and lovely you are!" he said. "I have never noticed before the beauty of your colors, morning-glory," and he let his warm glances fall and linger upon her.

The sunflower all this time changed into looking with jealous eyes, for she become the one who had continually welcomed the sun, and this morning he seemed to have completely forgotten her.

Still sunflower kept her gaze upon them and wondered what she could do to win back her king from the delicate little morning-glory.

But as she looked she saw the morning-glory sway and nod her head. "She is going to sleep," said the sunflower; "his warm breath makes her drowsy, or else she was up so early that she cannot keep awake."

While the sunflower watched, sure enough the morning-glory nodded and closed her eyes.

She was fast asleep, and the fickle sun, seeing that she no longer looked upon him, looked away and beheld the sunflower looking toward him with longing eyes.

"Good morning, King," she said, as she caught his eye, and she was wise enough not to let him know she had seen him before. So the sun smiled and turned his face upon them all, and the sunflower kept to herself what she had seen, knowing full well that she was the one who knew best how to keep his first and last glances.

A little later one of the flowers called out: "Look at morning-glory; she is still sleeping. Let us tell her it is time to awaken."

"Morning-glory! morning-glory!" they called, but she did not answer. She was sound asleep.

"That is strange," said the rose. "I wonder if she has gone to sleep never to awake. I have heard of such things happening."

After two or three mornings the other flowers ceased to notice morning- glory, for they thought she had ceased to be one of them, but the wise sunflower kept her own counsel. She knew that morning-glory had to sleep all day in order that she might not miss the sun; but, as I told you, she was wise enough not to complain, and she kept his love for her by so doing.

Dorothy and The Portrait

Dorothy was very fond of her grandmother and grandfather, and liked to visit them, but there were no little girls to play with, and sometimes she was lonely for someone her own age. She would wander about the house looking for the queer things that grandmothers always have in their homes.

The hall clocks interested Dorothy very much. It stood on the landing at the top of the stairs, and she used to sit and listen to its queer tick-tock and watch the hands, which moved with little nervous jumps.

Then there were on its face the stars and the moon and the sun, and they all were very wonderful to Dorothy. One day she went into the big parlor, where there were pictures of her grandfather and grandmother, and her great-grandfather and great-grandmother, also.

Dorothy thought the "greats" looked very sedate, and she felt sure they must have been very old to have been the parents of her grandfather.

But the picture that interested her the most was a large painting of three children, one a little girl about her own age, and one other older, and a boy, who wore queer-looking trousers, cut off below the knee. His suit was of black velvet, and he wore white stockings and black shoes.

The little girls were dressed in white, and their dresses had short sleeves and low necks. The older girl had black hair, but the one that Dorothy thought was her age had long, golden curls like hers, only the girl in the picture wore her hair parted, and the curls hung all about her face.

Dorothy climbed into a big chair and sat looking at them. "I wish they could play with me," she thought, and she smiled at the little golden-haired girl. And then, wonderful to tell, the girl in the picture smiled at Dorothy.

"Oh! are you alive?" asked Dorothy.

"Of course I am," the little girl replied. "I will come down, if you would like to have me, and visit with you."

"Oh, I should be so glad to have you!" Dorothy answered.

Then the boy stepped to the edge of the frame, and from there to the top of a big chair which stood under the picture, and stood in the chair seat. He held out his hand to the little girls and helped them to the floor in the courtliest manner. Dorothy got out of her chair and asked them to be seated, and the boy placed chairs for them beside her.

"What is your name?" asked the golden-haired girl, for she was the only one who spoke.

"That was my name," she said, when Dorothy told her. "I lived in this house," she continued, "and we used to have such good times. This is my sister and my brother." The little girl and boy smiled, but they let their sister do all the talking. "We used to roast chestnuts in the fireplace," she said, "and once we had a party in this room, and played all sorts of games."

Dorothy could not imagine that quiet room filled with children.

"Do you remember how we frightened poor old Uncle Zack in this room?" she said to her brother and sister, and then they all laughed.

"Do tell me about it," said Dorothy.

"These glass doors by the fireplace did not have curtains in our day," said the little girl, "and there were shells and other things from the ocean in one cupboard, and in the other there were a sword and a helmet and a pair of gauntlets.

My brother wrapped a sheet around him and put on the helmet and the gauntlets, and, taking the sword in his hand, he climbed into the cupboard and sat down. We ladies closed the doors and hid in the back of the sofa. Uncle Zack got here in to restore the fire, and my brother beckoned to him.

Poor Zack dropped the wood he was carrying and fell on his knees, trembling with fright. The door changed into now not fastened and my brother pushed it open and pointed the sword at poor Uncle Zack.

"'Don' hurt a po' ol' nigger,' stated Zack, very faintly."

'You told about the jam the children ate,' stated my brother, in a deep voice, 'and you already know you drank the remaining drop of rum Mammy Sue had for her rheumatism, and for this you must be punished,' and he brought the sword down on the floor of the cupboard with a bang.

"Poor Uncle Zack fell on his face with fright. This was too much for my sister and me, and we laughed out.

"You never saw any one change so quickly as Uncle Zack. He jumped up and we ran, but my brother had to get out of his disguise, and Uncle Zack caught him. He agreed not to tell our father if we did not tell about his fright, and so we escaped being punished."

"Tell me more about your life in this old house," said Dorothy, when the little girl finished her story. But just then the picture of Dorothy's great-grandmother moved and out she stepped from her frame. She walked with a very stately air toward the children and put her hand on the shoulder of the little girl who had been telling the story, and said: "You better go back to your frame now."

"Oh dear!" said the little girl. "I did so dislike being grown up, and I had forgotten all about it, when my grownup self reminds me. That is the trouble when you are in the room with your grown-up picture," she told Dorothy. "You see, I had to be so sedate after I married that I never even dared to think of my girlhood, but you come in here again someday and I will tell you more about the good times we had."

The boy mounted the chair first and helped his sisters back into the frame. Dorothy looked for her great-grandmother, but she, too, was back in her frame, looking as sedate as ever. The next day Dorothy asked her grandmother who the children were in the big picture.

"This one," she said, pointing to the little golden-haired girl, "was your great-grandmother; you were named for her; and the other little girl and boy were your grandfather's aunt and uncle. They were your great-great-aunt and uncle."

Dorothy did not pretty recognize the "great-great" a part of it, but she was happy to know that her stately-looking great-grandmother had as soon as been a little girl like her, hear more about the fun the children had in the days long ago.

Snow-White and Rose-Red

A poor widow once lived in a small house. In front of the cabin was a garden in which a rose tree grew; one of these white roses and the other was red.

She has two children, who look like roses. One was called Snow White and the other was a red rose. They were religious and loving, busy and stressful, like two children.

Snow White was the nicest and quietest of her sister who liked jumping in the fields, searching for flowers and hunting for summer birds. While Snow White stayed home with her mother, either help her work, or when she finishes reading aloud.

The two children were the greatest affection for each other. They were always looking hand in hand. And if Snow White tells her sister: "We will never separate", the other will respond, "We will not live long," the mother added: "What he has, always share it with the other."

They ran down in the woods, and picked up ripe berries. But not a single animal would have hurt them; on the contrary, everyone felt the highest esteem for small creatures.

The rabbit came to eat parsley from his hands, and the deer grazed beside it, and the deer did not notice; likewise, the birds did not move from the branch, but they sang in complete safety.

They had no misfortune; if they were enjoying in the woods, they lay on moss to rest and sleep until morning; her mother was satisfied with her safety, and she had no fear for them.

Once, when they spent the night in the woods, and the bright dawn woke on them, they saw a beautiful boy, in a snow white dress, shining like diamonds, and sitting near where they rested.

He got up when they opened their eyes and looked at them kindly; but he didn't say a word and went from the horizon to the woods.

When the children looked around, they saw that they were sleeping on the edge of the cliff, and they certainly would have fallen if they had gone two more steps in the dark. His mother said that a beautiful child should be the angel who takes care of the good children.

Snow White and Rose Red kept her mother's cabin so clean that it was a pleasure to look at her. In summer, the red rose came home, and every morning, before her mother woke up, she put a bouquet next to her bed. He had a rose from all rose bushes. In winter, Snow White lit the fire and lit the boiler, after polishing it until it turned gold.

At night, when the snow fell, his mother asked him to shut the door, then, when sitting at home, the righteous widow read a great book aloud as the girls turned.

Near them they draw a sheep, a white dove, with its head hidden under its wing, on the back of the barn.

One afternoon, when everyone was comfortably sitting together in this way, they knocked on the door, as if someone wanted to enter. "Hurry up, a red rose!" His mother said. "Open the door, and definitely the traveler who is taking refuge."

Red rose accordingly removed the bolt, hoping to see a poor man. But it wasn't any of that; he was a bear pushing his big head towards the open door.

The red rose screamed and jumped back, the sheep pumped, a dove raised its wings and Snow White hid behind her mother's bed. The bear started talking and said: "Do not be afraid: I will not harm you; I am half freezing and I would like to warm up a little before the fire." Poor bear! The mother replied: "Go in and lie on the fire; just beware that your hair does not burn."

Then he called Snow White a red rose, and told them that the bear was nice and that it wouldn't hurt them. They came, as I asked, and the lamb and dove soon approached without fear.

Children, begged the bear, "remove some snow from my coat." Then they brought the broom and poured the bear's coat completely clean. After that he stretched in front of the fire and was happy a little quiet, just to show that he was happy and comfortable.

Long ago, they were all good friends, and the kids started playing with their unexpected visitor, pulling their thick fur, putting their feet on their backs, or spinning it over and over again.

Then they took a thin branch of hazelnut, used it on its thick coat, and laughed when it wasted. The bear let them entertain this way, just sometimes screaming, when it went too far, "Kids, forgive me an inch of life!"

When it was night, and everyone was preparing to go to bed, the widow said to the bear: "You can stay here and lie next to the house, if you want, to protect yourself from the cold and bad weather." . "

The show was accepted, but when the morning came, and when it blew up in the east, the two children were allowed out, and returned to the snow in the woods.

After that, every night, meanwhile, the bear came, lay down on the fire and let the children play with him; so they became very fond of their playmate, and the door never closed at night until noon.

When spring came and everything began to look green and bright, one morning one told Snow White: "Now I have to leave you, and during the summer I will not be able to return."

"Where are you going, dear bear?" Snow White asked. "I have to go to the woods to protect my treasure from bad dwarves. In winter, when the earth is frozen, it must remain underground and impenetrable; but now that the sun's rays melted the earth, it can come to the surface, and anything that comes in their hands, Or they are taken to their caves, and rarely see the light of day again. " .

Snow White became very sad when he said goodbye to a good-mannered monster and opened the door in front of him to leave; but upon his departure he was caught by a hook on the lintel and tearing off a piece of his fur, Snow White believed that there was something shining like gold through the lease; but he went out so quickly She was not sure what it was and soon hid among the trees.

Mistress Pussy's Mistake

A very kind gentleman, who lived in a big house which was in the midst of a beautiful park, had a handsome cat of which he was very fond. While he felt sure Pussy was fond of him, he knew very well she would hurt the birds, so he put a pretty ribbon around Pussy's neck, and on it a little silver bell which tinkled every time she moved and this warned the birds that she was near.

Pussy resented this, but pretended she did now not care. One day a thrush was singing very sweetly on the bough of a tree which overhung a small lake.

Pussy walked along under the tree, and, searching up at the thrush, stated: "Madam Thrush, you have got a most stunning voice, and you are a totally handsome bird.

I do wish I were nearer to you, for I am not so young as I was once, and I cannot hear so well."

The thrush trilled a laugh at Pussy, and said: "Yes, Miss Puss,

I can well believe you want me nearer, however now not to peer or hear me better, however which you might draw close me."

Pussy pretended not to hear the last remark, but said: "My beautiful Thrush, will you not come down where I can hear you better? I cannot get about as nimbly as I used to when I was young, or I would go to you."

"I cannot sing so well on the ground," replied the thrush. "You can come up here, even if you are not so spry as you were. But tell me, do you not find the bell you wear very trying to your nerves?"

"Oh no," answered sly Pussy. "It is so pretty that I'm glad to wear it, and my master thinks I am so handsome that he likes to see me dressed well. And then he can always find me when he hears the bell. That is why I wear it." "I understand," answered the thrush, "and we bird are always glad to hear it, too." And she trilled another laugh at Pussy and added, "You are certainly a very handsome creature, Miss Puss."

Pussy all this time had very slowly climbed the tree, for she wanted the thrush to think she was old and slow, but the bird had her bright eyes upon her. When Pussy reached the branch the thrush was on she stopped and seated herself.

"Now, my pretty little friend, sing for me your loudest song."

She hoped it'd be loud sufficient to drown the tinkle of the bell.

The thrush commenced and become soon making a song very sweetly.

Pussy took a very cautious step and then remained quiet. The thrush stopped singing and spread her wings.

"Oh, do not stop!" said Puss. "Your song was so soothing I was in a doze; do sing again." And she moved a little closer.

The thrush took a step nearer to the end of the bough and said: "I am glad you like my voice. I will sing again if it pleases you so much."

She began her song, but she kept her eyes on Puss, and as Puss drew nearer she moved closer to the end of the swinging bough.

She had reached a very high note when Puss gave a spring, but the thrush was too quick; she flew out of Pussy's reach, and splash went Pussy into the lake, for she had not noticed that the thrush was moving to the end of the bough, so intent was she on the thought of catching her.

Poor Pussy was very wet when she scrambled to the bank of the lake, and the birds were chirping and making a great noise.

"How did you like your bath, Miss Puss?" the thrush called to her. "You should never lay traps for others, for often you fall into them yourself."

KID

Kid was one of those little boys who seemed to have grown up on the streets of the big city where he lived.

He never remembered a mother or a father, and no one ever took care of him. His first remembrance was of an old woman who gave him a crust of bread, and he slept in the corner of her room. One day they carried her away, and since then Kid had slept in a doorway or an alley.

By selling papers he managed to get enough to eat, and if he did not have the money he stole to satisfy his hunger.

He was often cold and hungry, but he saw many other children that were in the same condition, and he did not suppose that anyone ever had enough to eat or a warm place to sleep every night.

Kid went in to the Salvation Army meetings, when they held them in his neighborhood, because it was a place where the wind did not blow, and while there he heard them sing and talk about Some One who loved everybody and would help you if only you would ask Him. Kid was never able to find out just where this Person lived, and, therefore, he could not ask for help.

One-day Kid saw a lady who was too well dressed to belong in his part of the city, and he followed her, thinking that she might have a pocket-book he could take. The opportunity did not offer itself, however, and before Kid realized it he was in a part of the city he had never seen before.

The buildings were tall and the streets much cleaner than where he lived. Kid walked along, looking in windows of the stores, when he noticed a lady standing beside him with a jeweled watch hanging from her belt.

He had never seen anything so beautiful or so easy to take, and he waited for a few more people to gather around the window, and then he carefully reached.

For the watch, and with one pull off got here the trinket, and away ran Kid, like a deer, with the watch clasped firmly in his begrimed little hand.

On and on he ran, now not knowing in which he became going--nor caring, for that matter--and it appeared to Kid that the entire world become crying, "Stop, thief!" and become chasing him.

After a while the noise grew fainter and fainter and he stopped and looked back. There was not a person in sight.

Kid looked around him. All the houses were large with clean stone steps in front of them. Kid sat down on the bottom step of one of these houses and looked at his treasure.

He held it to his ear and heard its soft tick, then he looked at the sparkling stones on the case. He opened it and watched the little hands move, then he opened the back part, and there was the picture of a baby, a little boy, Kid thought. Around its chubby face have been curls, and its eyes were huge and earnest-looking. Kid sat watching at it for a few minutes, questioning who it turned into.

When he looked up he saw a large building across the street with a steeple on it, and on the top of that a cross.

The door of the building was open, and after a while Kid walked across the street and up the long, wide steps. He went in and looked cautiously about. It was still and no one was to be seen.

There were two doors, and Kid went to one of them and pushed it open. He thought for a minute he was dreaming, for he did not suppose that anything so grand could be real.

There were rows and rows of seats, and at the very end of the big room Kid saw a light. He walked down one of the aisles to in which the little flame turned into burning, and stood in front of the altar.

Kid looked at everything with a feeling of awe, but he had not the slightest idea of what it all meant, and he wondered who lived in this beautiful house, and thought it strange that no one appeared and told him to go out.

There were pictures on the wall and Kid came to one of a sweet-faced lady who was holding a little child. Kid started and stepped back as he looked at it. "It is the baby in the watch," he said. "This must be where he lives and that is his mother." Someone was coming. He became caught at final, he felt sure. He slid into a pew and crawled under the seat and saved very still--so still, in fact, that he fell asleep.

When he awoke a light was burning in the church and its rays fell across the picture of the mother and child in such a way that the eyes of the mother seemed to be looking straight at Kid under the seat.

For the first time in his life he felt like crying. "I wish I had a mother," he thought, "and I should like to have her hold me in her arms just as that little boy's mother is holding him. I would tell her about this watch and perhaps she would tell me how to get it back to the lady."

Kid crept from under the seat and stood up, and coming toward him down the aisle was a man. Kid thought he wore a queer-looking costume, and he dodged back of the seat; but the man had seen him and there was no use in trying to run away; besides that, Kid was not at all sure that he wished to get away.

"Is this your house?" asked Kid, when the man came up to him.

"No, my son," he replied; "this is the house of God."

Kid's heart leaped for joy; that was the name of the One the Salvation Army people told him about, who loved everybody and helped you.

"If you please," said Kid, "I should like to see Him."

The good man looked at Kid very earnestly, and then he said, "If you will tell me what you wish to see Him about, I am sure I can help you."

Kid told him about the watch and that he felt sure the lady lived there, as the baby in the big picture was very much like the picture in the watch. "And if this is God's house," said Kid, "I thought He might be the father and forgive me. I am very sorry that I took it."

The good man took Kid by the hand. "Come with me," he said; "you are forgiven, I am sure."

Kid was given a good supper, and for the first time in his life he slept in a real bed.

The next day the good man found the owner of the watch, and when she heard Kid's story she forgave him.

Kid was placed in a school, where he learned to be a good boy, as well as to be studious, and he soon forgot the old life. He grew to be a man of whom any mother could have been proud. But the only mother Kid ever knew was the mother of the little boy in the picture, which he cherishes as a thing sacred in his life.

Little China Doll

In a shop window sat a little China Doll. She had been in the store so long she could not remember ever living in any other place.

Long, long ago there were other china dolls, but one by one some little girl had carried them away and she was left alone. China Doll had black painted hair and big, staring eyes, and her lips and cheeks were very red. Her body was filled with sawdust and her hands and arms to the elbow were china, as were her feet and legs to her knees.

By and by wax dolls came to the store; they had real hair, all curls, and eyes that would open and close, and poor China Doll was set back in the window, and after a while she became installed a field at the shelf and taken out simplest as soon as a year--at Christmas-time--whilst she was dusted and put in the window again.

She felt very lonely with so many stylish wax dolls, and as she had given up hope of ever being chosen by any little girl, she was glad when the little old lady who kept the store put her back in the box on the shelf.

At last there came a time when the children no longer came to the store, but went to the big city for their toys, and China Doll and the little old storekeeper grew old together.

China Doll sat in the window all of the time now, with tape and thread and other beneficial things, but turned into the simplest thing little folk could want.

One day in summer a tally-ho stopped in front of the store, and a party of young people came in. They bought a number of things and filled the old store with their laughter. Suddenly the prettiest girl reached into the window and took out China Doll. "Oh, you dear, quaint little doll!" she said. "My grandmother has one just like this, girls, and I have asked her many times to give it to me to make a French pincushion, but she will not let me have it."

Oh, how China Doll's coronary heart beat! Could it be authentic that she turned into going at remaining? Yes, the quite female bought her and took her away at the tally-ho.

The subsequent day she dressed China Doll within the prettiest silk dress, this type of one as she had dreamed of years ago, with an overskirt and purled sleeves. Then she made her the dearest poke-bonnet trimmed with little roses. She also made her a pair of child boots.

When China Doll became all dressed the pretty girl positioned a ribbon over her arm, and on each stop turned into a bit bandbox. Then she stood China Doll on her dressing-table and used the little bins for pincushions.

And there, China Doll lived a very happy life, which teaches that all things come to those who wait.

Going Forward - Activating Your Parenting Imagination

When was the last time you talked about your imagination? What inspires you? What does bring you to life and envelop your mind with beauty? How can you start injecting an incredible space into the lives of your parents and family? I invite you to think about these questions and remain silent, perhaps even writing a diary as you begin to plan to share more surprises with your child.

After being surprised, you can take small steps every day to inject amazement into your experiences in everyday family life.

In this final chapter, I will share ideas to help you get started!

Create Moments to Live Off the Grid of Control and Predictability

First, we have to live by the control and prediction network. Where can you become a me in your life? Can you find a time when you don't live on calendars, digital, etc. and you simply enter a space without space without "cough" or "no's"? Reserve a time each week and then reserve a time each day to have a flexible thought about possible waves. Pause and allow you to use intrinsic motivation to guide you to what is coming.

Create a "TO BE" list for your week. Think of all the ways you can pause and practice right now. How can you stop? In what space of your days this week can you let yourself breathe, feel and observe the world around you? Is it made in nature?

Take a break every day and plan to start developing your "default automatic relaxation" skills at a special time with your child.

Spontaneity can be fun, especially during school holidays or on weekends. Can you plan a Sunday from time to time to allow Saturday to spread gracefully and easily in some way that inspires the day?

Adopt a heuristic mentality.

İnstead of answering the question, ask more, especially if it supports your child's learning. I know that children are growing up, you can often respond when it comes to problems. Looking back, you can see how fast you can jump to help, rescue or solve quickly, without realizing it you can send a message that I think you cannot answer alone.

Asking children questions helps them build confidence and also shows that adults believe in their ability and independence. Although it is surprising, in fact, to explore this wonderful world around us, one can only activate the discovery mentality with the intention of searching for that lens.

Every day, find ways of curiosity to open and expand your mind, thinking outside the box. When you make a family decision, brainstorm! Think of as many different solutions as possible and let wild and somewhat indirect ideas come to the table. This does not mean that I can finally continue with that solution, but the act of letting go of ideas is incredible.

Learn new things! Ask your child: what would you like to learn today that you have not thought of before? Here are some examples: bio-light, ancient Peru, groundhog habitats, unique deserts and sweet foods that are eaten throughout the world ... Talk about when you discover something really new and what you have learned, how you feel, talk about where and when did you find out.

Here are some tips to help you create a discovery mentality:

Open your mind to the secret of life.

It is likely to progress, move your compass to infinite possibilities.

Be compassionate with yourself While you walk the path of life, it is very beneficial to learn and grow!

Embrace the idea of "and" to "O": look for thought poles, black and white thinking and ways to navigate in the middle (less radical, slower, slower, steady, calm in thought and practice). Be.

Let nature show you its wonders.

The best advice when you start to create a wonderful atmosphere in your family life is to go out to nature and let the essence and the ways of being there show you what you fear.

Get up at dawn to listen to the birds! Get up early and go out with your baby to hear the chattering of the birds.

Walk barefoot on the grass.

Growth Mindset

We need to support our children to learn to think in ways that support their well-being and foster a sense of security and public welfare. In the world of education, the "growth mindset" is a common theme, and the growth mindset refers to this thought pattern.

How we think over time and how we teach our children ideas that make them feel good about risks, believe and focus on their strengths, try new things. Adopt a "failure", which involves seeing mistakes as learning. Opportunities, not reasons to embarrass or reflect on who they are as a person.

Positive Mentality

We can also develop mental training and curricula and expand them to teach positive patterns versus negative thinking patterns.

Most people agree that having a positive mental attitude, especially for children who exercise youth, is powerful. The discussion would be very difficult otherwise, and I am sure you agree. Youth sports programs should work hard to constantly promote a positive attitude. This can be done through careful training and teaching children to respect play and honesty in the field.

Create Your Positive Passports

The interesting thing about real passports was that children looked for the positive and helped them focus on the positive, which in turn boosted the positive interaction between them and at the same time created a positive atmosphere in the classroom.

During the year that students in a given area of the day needed some positive energy from "extra" thinking, the teacher allowed them to take their passports to that part of the day. For example, when several students struggled to stay on track and follow the instructions of teachers in music, he was forced to bring his passports to music so that the teacher could encourage positive thinking in class. It was a collaborative effort throughout the school day.

You can create your own passports with your child. Here's how to do it:

Then, I created, printed, cut and pasted my "Positive Passport" cover on the sheet. You can design yours with your baby to personalize it!

Finally, I used passports as a group activity to discuss the affirmation or positive thoughts we affirm about ourselves, positive conversation and how to use them as a place to record our positive actions throughout the day. We mark the points of kindness, the moments of use of our personal care tools and the comfort, exchange and delivery of others.

Conclusion

Taking your child to bed and staying in bed at night can be one of the most difficult things he does as a father. If you are one of the parents who knows what I am talking about, you should give up and let your child wake up because he cannot bear to cry, shout, hate or fight.

This can be a challenging time because as a father you have worked, cleaned, cooked and practiced almost everything a wonderful woman / man is expected to do in one day, and a little more! At the end of the day, all you have to do is stop a little "me." But you can't, because you have a "precious" self that wants to spend more time (or phone) with you. Trying to take them to bed is exhausting and messy! When you finally do this, it is difficult to completely relax because you are worried that he is about to go through the door again.

You love your child more than anything in the world, so there is nothing worse than seeing him restless or scared.

For years after my growth, my children realized that meditation and relaxation can help them sleep and help them sleep more deeply and more calmly. However, I probably didn't believe that such a simple and natural method would work very well, so I probably wouldn't try it.

Meditation at bedtime is when a child remembers his essential nature as focused, creative and peaceful, free to experience the joy of being fully present in that moment, now.

Sleep meditation for children implies the proper development of memory and the ability to concentrate, which will be especially useful for studying and pursuing their interests.

Meditation while sleeping helps your children relax without worrying about school and other activities so they can feel happy and comfortable.

Also, avoid eating large meals before bedtime to prevent children from feeling tired or asleep. Never let them force or breathe.

Let them look for a constant and gentle rhythmic breath that flows smoothly. If deep breathing causes dizziness, let them slow down or return to normal breathing.

I hope you enjoy reading this wonderful guide!

Printed in Poland
by Amazon Fulfillment
Poland Sp. z o.o., Wrocław